Contents

TUNA PASTA

Preparation Time : 10 minutes

Cooking Time : 8 minutes

Servings : 6

Difficulty Level : Average

INGREDIENTS:

- 10 oz can tuna, drained
- 15 oz whole wheat rotini pasta
- 4 oz mozzarella cheese, cubed
- 1/2 cup parmesan cheese, grated
- 1 tsp dried basil
- 14 oz can tomato
- 4 cups vegetable broth
- 1 tbsp garlic, minced
- 8 oz mushrooms, sliced
- 2 zucchinis, sliced
- 1 onion, chopped
- 2 tbsp olive oil
- Pepper
- Salt

DIRECTIONS:

1. Pour oil into the inner pot of instant pot and press the pot on sauté. Add mushrooms, zucchini, and onion and sauté until onion is softened. Add garlic and sauté for a minute.
2. Add pasta, basil, tuna, tomatoes, and broth and stir well. Seal and cook on high for 4 minutes. When completed, release pressure for 5 minutes then releases the remaining using quick release. Remove lid. Add remaining ingredients and stir well and serve.
3. **Nutrition (for 100g):** 346 Calories 9g Fat 3g Carbohydrates 3g Protein 830mg Sodium

AVOCADO AND TURKEY MIX PANINI

Preparation Time : 5 minutes

Cooking Time : 8 minutes

Servings : 2

Difficulty Level : Easy

INGREDIENTS:

* 2 red peppers, roasted and sliced into strips
* ¼ lb. thinly sliced mesquite smoked turkey breast
* 1 cup whole fresh spinach leaves, divided
* 2 slices provolone cheese
* 1 tbsp olive oil, divided
* 2 ciabatta rolls
* ¼ cup mayonnaise
* ½ ripe avocado

DIRECTIONS:

1. In a bowl, mash thoroughly together mayonnaise and avocado. Then preheat Panini press.
2. Chop the bread rolls in half and spread olive oil on the insides of the bread. Then fill it with filling, layering them as you go: provolone, turkey breast, roasted red pepper, spinach leaves and spread avocado mixture and cover with the other bread slice.
3. Place sandwich in the Panini press and grill for 5 to 8 minutes until cheese has melted and bread is crisped and ridged.

Nutrition (for 100g): 546 Calories 8g Fat 9g Carbohydrates 8g Protein 582mg Sodium

CUCUMBER, CHICKEN AND MANGO WRAP

Preparation Time : 5 minutes
Cooking Time : 20 minutes
Servings : 1
Difficulty Level : Difficult
INGREDIENTS:

* ½ of a medium cucumber cut lengthwise
* ½ of ripe mango
* 1 tbsp salad dressing of choice
* 1 whole wheat tortilla wrap
* 1-inch thick slice of chicken breast around 6-inch in length
* 2 tbsp oil for frying
* 2 tbsp whole wheat flour
* 2 to 4 lettuce leaves
* Salt and pepper to taste

DIRECTIONS:

1. Slice a chicken breast into 1-inch strips and just cook a total of 6-inch strips. That would be like two

strips of chicken. Store remaining chicken for future use.

2. Season chicken with pepper and salt. Dredge in whole wheat flour.
3. On medium fire, place a small and nonstick fry pan and heat oil. Once oil is hot, add chicken strips and fry until golden brown around 5 minutes per side.
4. While chicken is cooking, place tortilla wraps in oven and cook for 3 to 5 minutes. Then set aside and transfer in a plate.
5. Slice cucumber lengthwise, use only ½ of it and store remaining cucumber. Peel cucumber cut into quarter and remove pith. Place the two slices of cucumber on the tortilla wrap, 1-inch away from the edge.
6. Slice mango and store the other half with seed. Peel the mango without seed, slice into strips and place on top of the cucumber on the tortilla wrap.
7. Once chicken is cooked, place chicken beside the cucumber in a line.
8. Add cucumber leaf, drizzle with salad dressing of choice.
9. Roll the tortilla wrap, serve and enjoy.

Nutrition (for 100g): 434 Calories 10g Fat 65g Carbohydrates 21g Protein 691mg Sodium

FATTOUSH –MIDDLE EAST BREAD

Preparation Time : 10 minutes
Cooking Time : 15 minutes
Servings : 6
Difficulty Level : Difficult
INGREDIENTS:

- 2 loaves pita bread
- 1 tbsp Extra Virgin Olive Oil
- 1/2 tsp sumac, more for later
- Salt and pepper
- 1 heart of Romaine lettuce
- 1 English cucumber
- 5 Roma tomatoes
- 5 green onions
- 5 radishes
- 2 cups chopped fresh parsley leaves
- 1 cup chopped fresh mint leaves
- Dressing Ingredients:
- 1 1/2 lime, juice of

- 1/3 cup Extra Virgin Olive Oil
- Salt and pepper
- 1 tsp ground sumac
- 1/4 tsp ground cinnamon
- scant 1/4 tsp ground allspice

DIRECTIONS:

1. For 5 minutes toast the pita bread in the toaster oven. And then break the pita bread into pieces.
2. In a large pan on medium fire, heat 3 tbsp of olive oil in for 3 minutes. Add pita bread and fry until browned, around 4 minutes while tossing around.
3. Add salt, pepper and 1/2 tsp of sumac. Set aside the pita chips from the heat and put in paper towels to drain.
4. Toss well the chopped lettuce, cucumber, tomatoes, green onions, sliced radish, mint leaves and parsley in a large salad bowl.
5. To make the lime vinaigrette, whisk together all ingredients in a small bowl.
6. Stir in the dressing onto the salad and toss well. Mix in the pita bread.
7. Serve and enjoy.

Nutrition (for 100g): 192 Calories 8g Fats 1g Carbohydrates 9g Protein 655mg Sodium

WILTED DANDELION GREENS WITH SWEET ONION

Preparation Time : 15 minutes

Cooking Time : 15 minutes

Servings : 4

Difficulty Level : Easy

INGREDIENTS:

- 1 tablespoon extra-virgin olive oil
- 2 garlic cloves, minced
- 1 Vidalia onion, thinly sliced
- ½ cup low-sodium vegetable broth
- 2 bunches dandelion greens, roughly chopped
- Freshly ground black pepper, to taste

DIRECTIONS:

1. Heat up the olive oil in a large skillet over low heat. Add the garlic and onion and cook for 2 to 3 minutes, stirring occasionally, or until the onion is translucent.
2. Fold in the vegetable broth and dandelion greens and cook for 5 to 7 minutes until wilted, stirring

frequently. Sprinkle with the black pepper and serve on a plate while warm.

Nutrition (for 100g): 81 Calories 9g Fat 4g Carbohydrates 2g Protein 693mg Sodium

CELERY AND MUSTARD GREENS

Preparation Time : 10 minutes

Cooking Time : 15 minutes

Servings : 4

Difficulty Level : Average

INGREDIENTS:

- ½ cup low-sodium vegetable broth
- 1 celery stalk, roughly chopped
- ½ sweet onion, chopped
- ½ large red bell pepper, thinly sliced
- 2 garlic cloves, minced
- 1 bunch mustard greens, roughly chopped

DIRECTIONS:

1. Pour the vegetable broth into a large cast iron pan and bring it to a simmer over medium heat. Stir in the celery, onion, bell pepper, and garlic. Cook uncovered for about 3 to 5 minutes.
2. Add the mustard greens to the pan and stir well. Decrease heat and cook until the liquid is evaporated and the greens are wilted. Remove from the heat and serve warm.

Nutrition (for 100g): 39 Calories 1g Protein 8g Carbohydrates 3g Protein736mg Sodium

VEGETABLE AND TOFU SCRAMBLE

Preparation Time : 5 minutes

Cooking Time : 10 minutes

Servings : 2

Difficulty Level : Easy

INGREDIENTS:

- 2 tablespoons extra-virgin olive oil
- ½ red onion, finely chopped
- 1 cup chopped kale
- 8 ounces (227 g) mushrooms, sliced
- 8 ounces (227 g) tofu, cut into pieces
- 2 garlic cloves, minced

- Pinch red pepper flakes
- ½ teaspoon sea salt
- 1/8 teaspoon freshly ground black pepper

DIRECTIONS:

1. Cook the olive oil in a medium nonstick skillet over medium-high heat until shimmering. Add the onion, kale, and mushrooms to the skillet. Cook and stirring irregularly, or until the vegetables start to brown.
2. Add the tofu and stir-fry for 3 to 4 minutes until softened. Stir in the garlic, red pepper flakes, salt, and black pepper and cook for 30 seconds. Let it rest before serving.

Nutrition (for 100g): 233 Calories 9g Fat 2g Carbohydrates 4g Protein 733mg Sodium

ZUCCHINI-RICOTTA FRITTERS WITH LEMON-GARLIC AIOLI

Preparation Time : 10 minutes, plus 20 minutes rest time

Cooking Time : 25 minutes

Servings : 4

Difficulty Level : Difficult

INGREDIENTS:

- 1 large or 2 small/medium zucchini
- 1 teaspoon salt, divided
- ½ cup whole-milk ricotta cheese
- 2 scallions
- 1 large egg
- 2 garlic cloves, finely minced
- 2 tablespoons chopped fresh mint (optional)
- 2 teaspoons grated lemon zest
- ¼ teaspoon freshly ground black pepper
- ½ cup almond flour
- 1 teaspoon baking powder
- 8 tablespoons extra-virgin olive oil
- 8 tablespoons Roasted Garlic Aioli or avocado oil mayonnaise

DIRECTIONS:

1. Situate the shredded zucchini in a colander or on several layers of paper towels. Sprinkle with ½ teaspoon salt and let sit for 10 minutes. Using another layer of paper towel press down on the zucchini to release any excess moisture and pat dry. Incorporate the drained zucchini, ricotta, scallions, egg, garlic, mint (if using), lemon zest, remaining ½ teaspoon salt, and pepper.

2. Scourge together the almond flour and baking powder. Fold in the flour mixture into the zucchini mixture and let rest for 10 minutes. In a large skillet, working in four batches, fry the fritters. For each batch of four, heat 2 tablespoons olive oil over medium-high heat. Add 1 heaping tablespoon of zucchini batter per fritter, pressing down with the back of a spoon to form 2- to 3-inch fritters. Cover and let fry 2 minutes before flipping. Fry another 2 to 3 minutes, covered, or until crispy and golden and cooked through. You may need to reduce heat to medium to prevent burning. Remove from the pan and keep warm.

3. Repeat for the remaining three batches, using 2 tablespoons of the olive oil for each batch. Serve fritters warm with aioli.

Nutrition (for 100g): 448 Calories 42g Fat 2g Carbohydrates 8g Protein 744mg Sodium

SALMON-STUFFED CUCUMBERS

Preparation Time : 10 minutes

Cooking Time : 0 minutes

Servings : 4

Difficulty Level : Easy

INGREDIENTS:

- 2 large cucumbers, peeled
- 1 (4-ounce) can red salmon
- 1 medium very ripe avocado
- 1 tablespoon extra-virgin olive oil
- Zest and juice of 1 lime
- 3 tablespoons chopped fresh cilantro
- ½ teaspoon salt
- ¼ teaspoon freshly ground black pepper

DIRECTIONS:

1. Slice the cucumber into 1-inch-thick segments and using a spoon, scrape seeds out of center of each segment and stand up on a plate. In a medium bowl, mix the salmon, avocado, olive oil, lime zest and juice, cilantro, salt, and pepper and mix until creamy.

2. Scoop the salmon mixture into the center of each cucumber segment and serve chilled.

Nutrition (for 100g): 159 Calories 11g Fat 3g Carbohydrates 9g Protein 739mg Sodium

GOAT CHEESE–MACKEREL PÂTÉ

Preparation Time : 10 minutes

Cooking Time : 0 minutes

Servings : 4

Difficulty Level : Easy

INGREDIENTS:

- 4 ounces olive oil-packed wild-caught mackerel
- 2 ounces goat cheese
- Zest and juice of 1 lemon
- 2 tablespoons chopped fresh parsley
- 2 tablespoons chopped fresh arugula
- 1 tablespoon extra-virgin olive oil
- 2 teaspoons chopped capers
- 1 to 2 teaspoons fresh horseradish (optional)
- Crackers, cucumber rounds, endive spears, or celery, for serving (optional)

DIRECTIONS:

1. In a food processor, blender, or large bowl with immersion blender, combine the mackerel, goat cheese, lemon zest and juice, parsley, arugula, olive oil, capers, and horseradish (if using). Process or blend until smooth and creamy.
2. Serve with crackers, cucumber rounds, endive spears, or celery. Seal covered in the refrigerator for up to 1 week.

Nutrition (for 100g): 118 Calories 8g Fat 6g Carbohydrates 9g Protein 639mg Sodium

ZUCCHINI FETA ROULADES

Preparation Time : 10 minutes

Cooking Time : 10 minutes

Servings : 6

Difficulty Level : Average

INGREDIENTS:

- ½ cup feta
- 1 garlic clove, minced
- 2 tablespoons fresh basil, minced
- 1 tablespoon capers, minced
- 1/8 teaspoon salt
- 1/8 teaspoon red pepper flakes
- 1 tablespoon lemon juice
- 2 medium zucchinis
- 12 toothpicks

DIRECTIONS:

1. Preheat the air fryer to 360°F. (If using a grill attachment, make sure it is inside the air fryer during preheating.) In a small bowl, mix the feta, garlic, basil, capers, salt, red pepper flakes, and lemon juice.

2. Slice the zucchini into 1/8-inch strips lengthwise. (Each zucchini should yield around 6 strips.) Spread 1 tablespoon of the cheese filling onto each slice of zucchini, then roll it up and locked it with a toothpick through the middle.

3. Place the zucchini roulades into the air fryer basket in a one layer, individually. Bake or grill in the air fryer for 10 minutes. Remove the zucchini roulades from the air fryer and gently remove the toothpicks before serving.

Nutrition (for 100g): 46 Calories 3g Fat 6g Carbohydrates 3g Protein 710mg Sodium

GARLIC-ROASTED TOMATOES AND OLIVES

Preparation Time : 5 minutes

Cooking Time : 20 minutes

Servings : 6

Difficulty Level : Easy

INGREDIENTS:

- 2 cups cherry tomatoes
- 4 garlic cloves, roughly chopped
- ½ red onion, roughly chopped
- 1 cup black olives
- 1 cup green olives
- 1 tablespoon fresh basil, minced
- 1 tablespoon fresh oregano, minced
- 2 tablespoons olive oil
- ¼ to ½ teaspoon salt

DIRECTIONS:

1. Preheat the air fryer to 380°F. In a large bowl, incorporate all of the ingredients and toss together so that the tomatoes and olives are coated well with the olive oil and herbs.

2. Pour the mixture into the air fryer basket, and roast for 10 minutes. Stir the mixture well, then continue roasting for an additional 10 minutes. Remove from the air fryer, transfer to a serving bowl, and enjoy.

Nutrition (for 100g): 109 Calories 10g Fat 5g Carbohydrates 1g Protein 647mg Sodium

GOAT CHEESE AND GARLIC CROSTINI

Preparation Time : 3 minutes

Cooking Time : 5 minutes

Servings : 4

Difficulty Level : Average

INGREDIENTS:

- 1 whole wheat baguette
- ¼ cup olive oil
- 2 garlic cloves, minced
- 4 ounces goat cheese
- 2 tablespoons fresh basil, minced

DIRECTIONS:

1. Preheat the air fryer to 380°F. Cut the baguette into ½-inch-thick slices. In a small bowl, incorporate together the olive oil and garlic, then brush it over one side of each slice of bread.
2. Place the olive-oil-coated bread in a single layer in the air fryer basket and bake for 5 minutes. In the meantime, combine together the goat cheese and basil. Remove the toast from the air fryer, then spread a thin layer of the goat cheese mixture over on each piece and serve.

Nutrition (for 100g): 365 Calories 21g Fat 10g Carbohydrates 12g Protein 804mg Sodium

ROSEMARY-ROASTED RED POTATOES

Preparation Time : 5 minutes

Cooking Time : 20 minutes

Servings : 6

Difficulty Level : Easy

INGREDIENTS:

- 1-pound red potatoes, quartered
- ¼ cup olive oil
- ½ teaspoon kosher salt
- ¼ teaspoon black pepper
- 1 garlic clove, minced
- 4 rosemary sprigs

DIRECTIONS:

1. Preheat the air fryer to 360°F.
2. In a large bowl, toss in the potatoes with the olive oil, salt, pepper, and garlic until well coated. Fill the

air fryer basket with potatoes and top with the sprigs of rosemary.

3. Roast for 10 minutes, then stir or toss the potatoes and roast for 10 minutes more. Remove the rosemary sprigs and serve the potatoes. Season well.

Nutrition (for 100g): 133 Calories 9g Fat 5g Carbohydrates 1g Protein 617mg Sodium

AVOCADO EGG SCRAMBLE

Preparation Time : 8 minutes

Cooking Time : 15 minutes

Servings : 4

Difficulty Level : Average

INGREDIENTS:

- 4 eggs, beaten
- 1 white onion, diced
- 1 tablespoon avocado oil
- 1 avocado, finely chopped
- ½ teaspoon chili flakes
- 1 oz Cheddar cheese, shredded
- ½ teaspoon salt
- 1 tablespoon fresh parsley

DIRECTIONS:

1. Pour avocado oil in the skillet and bring it to boil. Then add diced onion and roast it until it is light brown. Meanwhile, mix up together chili flakes, beaten eggs, and salt.
2. Fill the egg mixture over the cooked onion and cook the mixture for 1 minute over the medium heat. After this, scramble the eggs well with the help of the fork or spatula. Cook the eggs until they are solid but soft.
3. After this, add chopped avocado and shredded cheese. Stir the scramble well and transfer in the serving plates. Sprinkle the meal with fresh parsley.

Nutrition (for 100g): 236 Calories 20g Fat 4g Carbohydrates 6g Protein 804mg Sodium

MORNING TOSTADAS

Preparation Time : 15 minutes

Cooking Time : 6 minutes

Servings : 6

Difficulty Level : Difficult

INGREDIENTS :

- ½ white onion, diced
- 1 tomato, chopped
- 1 cucumber, chopped
- 1 tablespoon fresh cilantro, chopped
- ½ jalapeno pepper, chopped
- 1 tablespoon lime juice
- 6 corn tortillas
- 1 tablespoon canola oil
- 2 oz Cheddar cheese, shredded
- ½ cup white beans, canned, drained
- 6 eggs
- ½ teaspoon butter
- ½ teaspoon Sea salt

DIRECTIONS:

1. Make Pico de Galo: in the salad bowl combine together diced white onion, tomato, cucumber, fresh cilantro, and jalapeno pepper. Then add lime juice and a ½ tablespoon of canola oil. Mix up the mixture well. Pico de Galo is cooked. After this, preheat the oven to 390F. Line the tray with baking paper. Arrange the corn tortillas on the baking paper and brush with remaining canola oil from both sides. Bake the tortillas until they start to be crunchy. Chill the cooked crunchy tortillas well. Meanwhile, toss the butter in the skillet.

2. Crack the eggs in the melted butter and sprinkle them with sea salt. Fry the eggs until the egg whites become white (cooked). Approximately for 3-5 minutes over the medium heat. After this, mash the beans until you get puree texture. Spread the bean puree on the corn tortillas. Add fried eggs. Then top the eggs with Pico de Galo and shredded Cheddar cheese.

Nutrition (for 100g): 246 Calories 11g Fat 7g Carbohydrates 7g Protein 593mg Sodium

PARMESAN OMELET

Preparation Time : 5 minutes
Cooking Time : 10 minutes
Servings : 2
Difficulty Level : Easy
INGREDIENTS:

- 1 tablespoon cream cheese
- 2 eggs, beaten
- ¼ teaspoon paprika

- ½ teaspoon dried oregano
- ¼ teaspoon dried dill
- 1 oz Parmesan, grated
- 1 teaspoon coconut oil

DIRECTIONS:

1. Mix up together cream cheese with eggs, dried oregano, and dill. Pour coconut oil in the skillet and heat it up until it will coat all the skillet. Then fill the skillet with the egg mixture and flatten it. Add grated Parmesan and close the lid. Cook omelet for 10 minutes over the low heat. Then transfer the cooked omelet in the serving plate and sprinkle with paprika.

Nutrition (for 100g): 148 Calories 5g Fat 3g Carbohydrates 6g Protein 741mg Sodium

WATERMELON PIZZA

Preparation Time : 10 minutes
Cooking Time : 0 minutes
Servings : 2
Difficulty Level : Easy
INGREDIENTS:

- 9 oz watermelon slice
- 1 tablespoon Pomegranate sauce
- 2 oz Feta cheese, crumbled
- 1 tablespoon fresh cilantro, chopped

DIRECTIONS:

1. Place the watermelon slice in the plate and sprinkle with crumbled Feta cheese. Add fresh cilantro. After this, sprinkle the pizza with Pomegranate juice generously. Cut the pizza into the servings.

Nutrition (for 100g): 143 Calories 2g Fat 6g Carbohydrates 1g Protein 811mg Sodium

SAVORY MUFFINS

Preparation Time : 10 minutes
Cooking Time : 15 minutes
Servings : 4
Difficulty Level : Average
INGREDIENTS:

- 3 oz ham, chopped
- 4 eggs, beaten
- 2 tablespoons coconut flour

- ½ teaspoon dried oregano
- ¼ teaspoon dried cilantro
- Cooking spray

DIRECTIONS:

1. Spray the muffin's molds with cooking spray from inside. In the bowl mix up together beaten eggs, coconut flour, dried oregano, cilantro, and ham. When the liquid is homogenous, pour it in the prepared muffin molds.
2. Bake the muffins for 15 minutes at 360F. Chill the cooked meal well and only after this remove from the molds.

Nutrition (for 100g): 128 Calories 2g Fat 9g Carbohydrates 1g Protein 882mg Sodium

MORNING PIZZA WITH SPROUTS

Preparation Time : 15 minutes
Cooking Time : 20 minutes
Servings : 6
Difficulty Level : Average
INGREDIENTS :

- ½ cup wheat flour, whole grain
- 2 tablespoons butter, softened
- ¼ teaspoon baking powder
- ¾ teaspoon salt
- 5 oz chicken fillet, boiled
- 2 oz Cheddar cheese, shredded
- 1 teaspoon tomato sauce
- 1 oz bean sprouts

DIRECTIONS :

1. Make the pizza crust: mix up together wheat flour, butter, baking powder, and salt. Knead the soft and non-sticky dough. Add more wheat flour if needed. Leave the dough for 10 minutes to chill. Then place the dough on the baking paper. Cover it with the second baking paper sheet.
2. Roll up the dough with the help of the rolling pin to get the round pizza crust. After this, remove the upper baking paper sheet. Transfer the pizza crust in the tray.
3. Spread the crust with tomato sauce. Then shred the chicken fillet and arrange it over the pizza crust. Add shredded Cheddar cheese. Bake pizza for 20 minutes at 355F. Then top the cooked pizza with bean sprouts and slice into the servings.

Nutrition (for 100g): 157 Calories 8g Fat 3g Carbohydrates 5g Protein 753mg Sodium

BANANA QUINOA

Preparation Time : 10 minutes

Cooking Time : 12 minutes

Servings : 4

Difficulty Level : Easy

INGREDIENTS:

- 1 cup quinoa
- 2 cup milk
- 1 teaspoon vanilla extract
- 1 teaspoon honey
- 2 bananas, sliced
- ¼ teaspoon ground cinnamon

DIRECTIONS:

1. Pour milk in the saucepan and add quinoa. Close the lid and cook it over the medium heat for 12 minutes or until quinoa will absorb all liquid. Then chill the quinoa for 10-15 minutes and place in the serving mason jars.
2. Add honey, vanilla extract, and ground cinnamon. Stir well. Top quinoa with banana and stirs it before serving.

Nutrition (for 100g): 279 Calories 3g Fat 6g Carbohydrates 7g Protein 581mg Sodium

BLUEBERRY COMPOTE

Preparation Time : 10 minutes

Cooking Time : 0 minutes

Servings : 8

Difficulty Level : Average

INGREDIENTS:

- 1 (16-ounce) bag frozen blueberries, thawed
- ¼ cup sugar
- 1 tablespoon lemon juice
- 2 tablespoons cornstarch
- 2 tablespoons water
- ¼ teaspoon vanilla extract
- ¼ teaspoon grated lemon zest

DIRECTIONS:

1. Add blueberries, sugar, and lemon juice to the Instant Pot. Cover and press the Manual button, and adjust time to 1 minute.
2. When the timer beeps, sharply-release the pressure until the float valve falls. Press the Cancel button and open it.
3. Press the Sauté button. Combine cornstarch and water. Stir into blueberry mixture and cook until mixture comes to a boil and thickens, about 3–4 minutes. Press the Cancel button and stir in vanilla and lemon zest. Serve immediately or refrigerate until ready to serve.

Nutrition (for 100g): 57 Calories 2g Fat 14g Carbohydrates 7g Protein 348mg Sodium

DRIED FRUIT COMPOTE

Preparation Time : 5 minutes
Cooking Time : 20 minutes
Servings : 6
Difficulty Level : Average
INGREDIENTS:

- 8 ounces dried apricots, quartered
- 8 ounces dried peaches, quartered
- 1 cup golden raisins
- 1½ cups orange juice
- 1 cinnamon stick
- 4 whole cloves

DIRECTIONS:

1. Stir to merge. Close, select the Manual button, and adjust the time to 3 minutes. When the timer beeps, let pressure release naturally, about 20 minutes. Press the Cancel button and open lid.
2. Remove and discard cinnamon stick and cloves. Press the Sauté button and simmer for 5–6 minutes. Serve warm then cover and refrigerate for up to a week.

Nutrition (for 100g): 258 Calories 5g Fat 8g Carbohydrates 4g Protein 277mg Sodium

CHOCOLATE RICE PUDDING

Preparation Time : 10 minutes
Cooking Time : 20 minutes
Servings : 6
Difficulty Level : Easy
INGREDIENTS:

- 2 cups almond milk

- 1 cup long-grain brown rice
- 2 tablespoons Dutch-processed cocoa powder
- ¼ cup maple syrup
- 1 teaspoon vanilla extract
- ½ cup chopped dark chocolate

DIRECTIONS:

1. Place almond milk, rice, cocoa, maple syrup, and vanilla in the Instant Pot. Close then select the Manual button, and set time to 20 minutes. When the timer beeps, let pressure release naturally for 15 minutes, then quick-release the remaining pressure. Press the Cancel button and open lid. Serve warm, sprinkled with chocolate.

Nutrition (for 100g): 271 Calories 8g Fat 4g Carbohydrates 3g Protein 360mg Sodium

FRUIT COMPOTE

Preparation Time : 10 minutes

Cooking Time : 15 minutes

Servings : 6

Difficulty Level : Average

INGREDIENTS:

- 1 cup apple juice
- 1 cup dry white wine
- 2 tablespoons honey
- 1 cinnamon stick
- ¼ teaspoon ground nutmeg
- 1 tablespoon grated lemon zest
- 1½ tablespoons grated orange zest
- 3 large apples, peeled, cored, and chopped
- 3 large pears, peeled, cored, and chopped
- ½ cup dried cherries

DIRECTIONS:

1. Situate all ingredients in the Instant Pot and stir well. Close and select the Manual button, and allow to sit for 1 minute. When the timer beeps, rapidly-release the pressure until the float valve hit the bottom. Click the Cancel then open lid.

2. Use a slotted spoon to transfer fruit to a serving bowl. Remove and discard cinnamon stick. Press the Sauté button and bring juice in the pot to a boil. Cook, stirring constantly, until reduced to a syrup that will coat the back of a spoon, about 10 minutes.

3. Stir syrup into fruit mixture. Once cool slightly, then wrap with plastic and chill overnight.

Nutrition (for 100g): 211 Calories 1g Fat 4g Carbohydrates 2g Protein 208mg Sodium

STUFFED APPLES

Preparation Time : 10 minutes

Cooking Time : 15 minutes

Servings : 6

Difficulty Level : Difficult

INGREDIENTS:

- ½ cup apple juice
- ¼ cup golden raisins
- ¼ cup chopped toasted walnuts
- 2 tablespoons sugar
- ½ teaspoon grated orange zest
- ½ teaspoon ground cinnamon
- 4 large cooking apples
- 4 teaspoons unsalted butter
- 1 cup water

DIRECTIONS:

1. Put apple juice in a microwave-safe container; heat for 1 minute on high or until steaming and hot. Pour over raisins. Soak raisins for 30 minutes. Drain, reserving apple juice. Add nuts, sugar, orange zest, and cinnamon to raisins and stir to mix.

2. Cut off the top fourth of each apple. Peel the cut portion and chop it, then stir diced apple pieces into raisin mixture. Hollow out and core apples by cutting to, but not through, the bottoms.

3. Situate each apple on a piece of aluminum foil that is large enough to wrap apple completely. Fill apple centers with raisin mixture.

4. Top each with 1 teaspoon butter. Cover the foil around each apple, folding the foil over at the top and then pinching it firmly together.

5. Stir in water to the Instant Pot and place rack inside. Place apples on the rack. Close lid, set steam release to Sealing, press the Manual, and alarm to 10 minutes.

6. When the timer beeps, quick-release the pressure until the float valve drops and open the lid. Carefully lift apples out of the Instant Pot. Unwrap and transfer to plates. Serve hot, at room temperature, or cold.

Nutrition (for 100g): 432 Calories 16g Fat 6g Carbohydrates 3g Protein 361mg Sodium

CINNAMON-STEWED DRIED PLUMS

WITH GREEK YOGURT

Preparation Time : 10 minutes

Cooking Time : 15 minutes

Servings : 6

Difficulty Level : Easy

INGREDIENTS:

- 3 cups dried plums
- 2 cups water
- 2 tablespoons sugar
- 2 cinnamon sticks
- 3 cups low-fat plain Greek yogurt

DIRECTIONS:

1. Add dried plums, water, sugar, and cinnamon to the Instant Pot. Close allow steam release to Sealing, press the Manual button, and start the time to 3 minutes.
2. Once the timer beeps, quick-release the pressure. Click the Cancel button and open. Remove and discard cinnamon sticks. Serve warm over Greek yogurt.

Nutrition (for 100g): 301 Calories 2g Fat 3g Carbohydrates 14g Protein 244mg Sodium

VANILLA-POACHED APRICOTS

Preparation Time : 10 minutes

Cooking Time : 20 minutes

Servings : 6

Difficulty Level : Average

INGREDIENTS:

- 1¼ cups water
- ¼ cup marsala wine
- ¼ cup sugar
- 1 teaspoon vanilla bean paste
- 8 medium apricots, sliced in half and pitted

DIRECTIONS:

1. Place all pieces in the Instant Pot and combine well. Seal tight, click the Manual Instant Pot. Stir to combine. Close lid, set steam release to Sealing, press the Manual button, and set second to 1 minute.
2. When the alarm beeps, quick-release the pressure until the float valve drops. Set the Cancel and open lid. Let stand for 10 minutes. Carefully remove apricots from poaching liquid with a slotted spoon.

Serve warm or at room temperature.

Nutrition (for 100g): 62 Calories 1g Fat 5g Carbohydrates 2g Protein 311mg Sodium

CREAMY SPICED ALMOND MILK

Preparation Time : 10 minutes

Cooking Time : 15 minutes

Servings : 6

Difficulty Level : Average

INGREDIENTS:

- 1 cup raw almonds
- 5 cups filtered water, divided
- 1 teaspoon vanilla bean paste
- ½ teaspoon pumpkin pie spice

DIRECTIONS:

1. Stir in almonds and 1 cup water to the Instant Pot. Close and select the Manual, and set time to 1 minute.
2. When the timer alarms, quick-release the pressure until the float valve drops. Click the Cancel button and open cap. Strain almonds and rinse under cool water. Transfer to a high-powered blender with remaining 4 cups water. Purée for 2 minutes on high speed.
3. Incorporate mixture into a nut milk bag set over a large bowl. Squeeze bag to extract all liquid. Stir in vanilla and pumpkin pie spice. Transfer to a Mason jar or sealed jug and refrigerate for 8 hours. Stir or shake gently before serving.

Nutrition (for 100g): 86 Calories 8g Fat 5g Carbohydrates 3g Protein 259mg Sodium

POACHED PEARS WITH GREEK YOGURT AND PISTACHIO

Preparation Time : 10 minutes

Cooking Time : 15 minutes

Servings : 8

Difficulty Level : Average

INGREDIENTS:

- 2 cups water
- 1¾ cups apple cider
- ¼ cup lemon juice
- 1 cinnamon stick

- 1 teaspoon vanilla bean paste
- 4 large Bartlett pears, peeled
- 1 cup low-fat plain Greek yogurt
- ½ cup unsalted roasted pistachio meats

DIRECTIONS:

1. Add water, apple cider, lemon juice, cinnamon, vanilla, and pears to the Instant Pot. Close lid, set steam release, switch the Manual, and set time to 3 minutes.
2. When the timer stops, swift-release the pressure until the float valve drops. Select the Cancel button and open cap. Take out pears to a plate and allow to cool to room temperature.
3. To serve, carefully slice pears in half with a sharp paring knife and scoop out core with a melon baller. Lay pear halves on dessert plates or in shallow bowls. Top with yogurt and garnish with pistachios. Serve immediately.

Nutrition (for 100g): 181 Calories 7g Fat 5g Carbohydrates 7g Protein 253mg Sodium

PEACHES POACHED IN ROSE WATER

Preparation Time : 10 minutes
Cooking Time : 20 minutes
Servings : 6
Difficulty Level : Average
INGREDIENTS:

- 1 cup water
- 1 cup rose water
- ¼ cup wildflower honey
- 8 green cardamom pods, lightly crushed
- 1 teaspoon vanilla bean paste
- 6 large yellow peaches, pitted and quartered
- ½ cup chopped unsalted roasted pistachio meats

DIRECTIONS:

1. Add water, rose water, honey, cardamom, and vanilla to the Instant Pot. Whisk well, then add peaches. Close lid, allow to steam release to Seal, press the Manual button, and alarm time to 1 minute.
2. When done, release the pressure until the float valve hits the bottom. Press the Remove and open it. Allow peaches to stand for 10 minutes. Carefully remove peaches from poaching liquid with a slotted spoon.
3. Slip skins from peach slices. Arrange slices on a plate and garnish with pistachios. Serve warm or at room temperature.

Nutrition (for 100g): 145 Calories 3g Fat 6g Carbohydrates 2g Protein 281mg Sodium

BROWN BETTY APPLE DESSERT

Preparation Time : 10 minutes

Cooking Time : 10 minutes

Servings :

Difficulty Level : Difficult

INGREDIENTS:

- 2 cups dried bread crumbs
- ½ cup sugar
- 1 teaspoon ground cinnamon
- 3 tablespoons lemon juice
- 1 tablespoon grated lemon zest
- 1 cup olive oil, divided
- 8 medium apples, peeled, cored, and diced
- 2 cups water

DIRECTIONS:

1. Combine crumbs, sugar, cinnamon, lemon juice, lemon zest, and ½ cup oil in a medium mixing bowl. Set aside.
2. In a greased oven-safe dish that will fit in your cooker loosely, add a thin layer of crumbs, then one diced apple. Continue filling the container with alternating layers of crumbs and apples until all ingredients are finished. Pour remaining ½ cup oil on top.
3. Pour water to the Instant Pot and place rack inside. Make a foil sling by folding a long piece of foil in half lengthwise and lower the uncovered container into the pot using the sling.
4. Seal and press the Manual button, and set time to 10 minutes. When the timer stops, let pressure release naturally, about 20 minutes. Press the Cancel button and open lid. Using the sling, remove the baking dish from the pot and let stand for 5 minutes before serving.

Nutrition (for 100g): 422 Calories 27g Fat 4g Carbohydrates 7g Protein 355mg Sodium

BLUEBERRY OAT CRUMBLE

Preparation Time : 10 minutes

Cooking Time : 10 minutes

Servings : 8

Difficulty Level : Difficult

INGREDIENTS:

- 1 cup water

- 4 cups blueberries
- 2 tablespoons packed light brown sugar
- 2 tablespoons cornstarch
- 1/8 teaspoon ground nutmeg
- 1/3 cup rolled oats
- ¼ cup granulated sugar
- ¼ cup all-purpose flour
- ¼ teaspoon ground cinnamon
- ¼ cup unsalted butter, melted and cooled

DIRECTIONS:

1. Brush baking dish that fits inside the Instant Pot with nonstick cooking spray. Add water to the pot and add rack. Crease a long piece of aluminum foil in half lengthwise. Lay foil over rack to form a sling.
2. In a medium bowl, combine blueberries, brown sugar, cornstarch, and nutmeg. Transfer mixture to prepared dish.
3. In a separate medium bowl, add oats, sugar, flour, and cinnamon. Mix well. Add butter and combine until mixture is crumbly. Sprinkle crumbles over blueberries, cover dish with aluminum foil, and crimp edges tightly.
4. Add baking dish to rack in pot so it rests on the sling and seal tight. Switch the Manual button, and set time to 10 minutes. When the timer beeps, let pressure release naturally for 10 minutes, then quick-release the remaining pressure until the float valve drops. Press the Cancel button and open lid. Carefully remove dish with sling and remove foil cover.
5. Heat broiler on high. Broil crumble until topping is golden brown, about 5 minutes. Serve warm or at room temperature.

Nutrition (for 100g): 159 Calories 6g Fat 3g Carbohydrates 2g Protein 477mg Sodium

DATE AND WALNUT COOKIES

Preparation Time : 10 minutes
Cooking Time : 2 minutes
Servings : 30
Difficulty Level : Average
INGREDIENTS:

- 2 cups flour
- 1/4 cup sour cream
- 1/2 cup butter, softened
- 1 1/2 cups brown sugar

- 1/2 cup white sugar
- 1 egg
- 1 cup dates, pitted and chopped
- 1/3 cup water
- 1/4 cup walnuts, finely chopped
- 1/2 tsp salt
- 1/2 tsp baking soda
- a pinch of cinnamon

DIRECTIONS:

1. Cook the dates together with the white sugar and water over medium-high heat, stirring constantly, until mixture is thick like jam. Add in the nuts, stir and remove from heat. Leave to cool.

2. In a medium bowl, scourge the butter and brown sugar. Stir in the egg and the sour cream. Mix the flour together with salt, baking soda and cinnamon and stir it into the butter mixture. Drop a teaspoon of dough onto a cookie sheet, place 1/4 teaspoon of the filling on top of it and top with an additional 1/2 teaspoon of dough. Repeat with the rest of the dough. Bake cookies for about 10 minutes in a preheated to 340 F oven, or until golden.

Nutrition (for 100g): 134 Calories 9g Fats 2g Carbohydrates 4g Protein 341mg Sodium

MOROCCAN STUFFED DATES

Preparation Time : 15 minutes
Cooking Time : 0 minutes
Servings : 30
Difficulty Level : Easy
INGREDIENTS:

- 1 lb. dates
- 1 cup blanched almonds
- 1/4 cup sugar
- 1 1/2 tbsp orange flower water
- 1 tbsp butter, melted
- 1/4 teaspoon cinnamon

DIRECTIONS:

1. Incorporate the almonds, sugar and cinnamon in a food processor. Stir in the butter and orange flower water and process until a smooth paste is formed. Roll small pieces of almond paste the same length as a date. Take one date, make a vertical cut and discard the pit. Insert a piece of the almond paste and press the sides of the date firmly around. Repeat with all the remaining dates and almond paste.

Nutrition (for 100g): 102 Calories 7g Fats 5g Carbohydrates 2g Protein 310mg Sodium

FIG COOKIES

Preparation Time : 10 minutes

Cooking Time : 15 minutes

Servings : 24

Difficulty Level : Average

INGREDIENTS:

- 1 cup flour
- 1 egg
- 1/2 cup sugar
- 1/2 cup figs, chopped
- 1/2 cup butter
- 1/4 cup water
- 1/2 tsp vanilla extract
- 1 tsp baking powder
- a pinch of salt

DIRECTIONS:

1. Cook figs with water, stirring, for 4-5 minutes, or until thickened. Set aside to cool. Scourge butter with sugar until light and fluffy. Put in the egg and vanilla and beat to blend well. In separate bowl, incorporate together flour, baking powder and salt. Blend this into the egg mixture. Stir in the cooled figs.

2. Drop teaspoonfuls of dough on a greased baking tray. Bake in a preheated to 375 degrees F oven until lightly browned. Remove cookies and cool on wire racks.

Nutrition (for 100g): 111 Calories 9g Fats 5g Carbohydrates 3g Protein 253mg Sodium

ALMOND COOKIES

Preparation Time : 10 minutes

Cooking Time : 15 minutes

Servings : 30

Difficulty Level : Easy

INGREDIENT:

- 1 cup almonds, blanched, toasted and finely chopped
- 1 cup powdered sugar
- 4 egg whites

- 2 tbsp flour
- 1/2 tsp vanilla extract
- 1 pinch ground cinnamon
- powdered sugar, to dust

DIRECTIONS:

1. Preheat oven to 320 F. Blend the almonds in a food processor until finely chopped. Beat egg whites and sugar until thick. Add in vanilla extract and cinnamon. Gently stir in almonds and flour. Place tablespoonfuls of mixture on two lined baking trays. Bake for 10 minutes, or until firm. Turn it off, and leave cookies to cool. Dust with powdered sugar.

Nutrition (for 100g): 106 Calories 6g Fats 7g Carbohydrates 1g Protein 214mg Sodium

TURKISH DELIGHT COOKIES

Preparation Time : 5 minutes

Cooking Time : 20 minutes

Servings : 48

Difficulty Level : Difficult

INGREDIENTS:

- 4 cups flour
- 3/4 cup sugar
- 1 cup lard (or butter)
- 3 eggs
- 1 tsp baking powder
- 1 tsp vanilla extract
- 8 oz Turkish delight, chopped
- powdered sugar, for dusting

DIRECTIONS:

1. Ready oven to 375 F. Put parchment paper onto the baking sheet. Beat the eggs well, adding sugar a bit at a time. Beat for at least 3 minutes. Melt the lard, then let it cool enough and slowly combine it with the egg mixture.

2. Mix the flour and the baking powder. Lightly add the flour mixture to the egg and lard mixture to create a smooth dough. Divide dough into two or three smaller balls and roll it out until ¼ inch thick. Cut squares 3x2 inch. Situate a piece of Turkish delight in each square, roll each cookie into a stick and nip the end. Bake in a preheated to 350 degrees F oven until light pink. Dust in powdered sugar and store in an airtight container when completely cool.

Nutrition (for 100g): 109 Calories 7g Fats 5g Carbohydrates 3g Protein 205mg Sodium

ANISE COOKIES

Preparation Time : 10 minutes
Cooking Time : 20 minutes
Servings : 24
Difficulty Level : Average
INGREDIENTS:

- 1 ½ cups flour
- 1/3 cup sugar
- 1/3 cup olive oil
- 1 egg, whisked
- 3 tsp fennel seeds
- 1 tsp cinnamon
- zest of one orange
- 3 tbsp anise liqueur
- sugar, for sprinkling

DIRECTIONS:

1. Cook olive oil in a small pan and sauté fennel seeds for 20-30 seconds. In a large bowl, combine together flour, sugar, and cinnamon. Add in olive oil, stirring, until well combined. Add orange zest and anise liqueur. Mix well then knead with hands until a smooth dough is formed. Add a little water if necessary.
2. On a well-floured surface, form two 1-inch long logs. Cut 1/8-inch cookies, arrange them on greased baking sheets. Egg wash each cookie and sprinkle with sugar. Bake cookies in a preheated to 350 F oven, for about 10 minutes, or until golden and crisp. Once cool, put in an airtight container.

Nutrition (for 100g): 113 Calories 8g Fats 5g Carbohydrates 2g Protein 255mg Sodium

SPANISH NOUGAT

Preparation Time : 5 minutes
Cooking Time : 20 minutes
Servings : 24
Difficulty Level : Average
INGREDIENTS:

- 11/2 cup honey
- 3 egg whites
- 1 ¾ cup almonds, roasted and chopped

DIRECTIONS:

1. Put the honey into a saucepan and boil over medium-high heat, then set aside to cool. Beat the egg whites to a thick glossy meringue and fold them into the honey. Bring the mixture back to medium-high heat and let it simmer, constantly stirring, for 15 minutes. When the color and consistency change to dark caramel, remove from heat, add the almonds and mix trough.

2. Put foil in a 9x13 inch pan and pour the hot mixture on it. Cover with another piece of foil and even out. Let cool completely. Place a wooden board weighted down with some heavy cans on it. Leave like this for 3-4 days, so it hardens and dries out. Slice into 1-inch squares.

Nutrition (for 100g): 110 Calories 5g Fats 7g Carbohydrates 1g Protein 336mg Sodium

PENNETTE WITH SALMON AND VODKA

Preparation Time : 10 minutes

Cooking Time : 18 minutes

Servings : 4

Difficulty Level : Easy

INGREDIENTS:

- 14oz Pennette Rigate
- 7oz Smoked salmon
- 2oz Shallot
- 35 fl. oz(40ml) Vodka
- 5 oz cherry tomatoes
- 7 oz fresh liquid cream (I recommend the vegetable one for a lighter dish)
- Chives to taste
- 3 tablespoons extra virgin olive oil
- Salt to taste
- Black pepper to taste
- Basil to taste (for garnish)

DIRECTIONS:

1. Wash and cut the tomatoes and the chives. After having peeled the shallot, chop it with a knife, put it in a saucepan and let it marinate in extra virgin olive oil for a few moments.

2. Meanwhile, cut the salmon into strips and sauté it together with the oil and shallot.

3. Blend everything with the vodka, being careful as there could be a flare (if a flame should rise, don't worry, it will lower as soon as the alcohol has evaporated completely). Add the chopped tomatoes and add a pinch of salt and, if you like, some pepper. Finally, add the cream and chopped chives.

4. While the sauce continues cooking, prepare the pasta. Once the water boils, pour in the Pennette and let them cook until al dente.

5. Strain the pasta, and pour the Pennette into the sauce, letting them cook for a few moments so as allow them to absorb all the flavor. If you like, garnish with a basil leaf.

Nutrition (for 100g): 620 Calories 9g Fat 7g Carbohydrates 24g Protein 326mg Sodium

SEAFOOD CARBONARA

Preparation Time : 15 minutes

Cooking Time : 50 minutes

Servings : 3

Difficulty Level : Easy

INGREDIENTS:

- 5oz Spaghetti
- 5oz Tuna
- 5oz Swordfish
- 5oz Salmon
- 6 Yolks
- 4 tablespoons Parmesan cheese (Parmigiano Reggiano)
- 2 fl. oz (60ml) White wine
- 1 clove garlic
- Extra virgin olive oil to taste
- Table Salt to taste
- Black pepper to taste

DIRECTIONS:

1. Prepare a boiling water in a pot and add a little salt.
2. Meanwhile, pour 6 egg yolks in a bowl and add the grated parmesan, pepper and salt. Beat with a whisk, and dilute with a little cooking water from the pot.
3. Remove any bones from the salmon, the scales from the swordfish, and proceed by dicing the tuna, salmon and swordfish.
4. Once it boils, toss in the pasta and cook it slightly al dente.
5. Meanwhile, heat a little oil in a large pan, add the whole peeled garlic clove. Once the oil is hot, toss in the fish cubes and sauté over high heat for about 1 minute. Remove the garlic and add the white wine.
6. Once the alcohol evaporates, take out the fish cubes and lower the heat. As soon as the spaghetti are ready, add them to the pan and sauté for about a minute, stirring constantly and adding the cooking water, as needed.
7. Pour in the egg yolk mixture and the fish cubes. Mix well. Serve.

Nutrition (for 100g): 375 Calories 17g Fat 40g Carbohydrates 14g Protein 755 mg Sodium

GARGANELLI WITH ZUCCHINI PESTO AND SHRIMP

Preparation Time : 10 minutes

Cooking Time : 30 minutes

Servings : 4

Difficulty Level : Average

INGREDIENTS:

* 14 oz egg-based Garganelli
* For the zucchini pesto:
* 7oz Zucchini
* 1 cup Pine nuts
* 8 tablespoons (35oz) Basil
* 1 teaspoon of table Salt
* 9 tablespoons extra virgin olive oil
* 2 tablespoons Parmesan cheese to be grated
* 1oz of Pecorino to be grated
* For the sautéed shrimp:
* 8oz shrimp
* 1 clove garlic
* 7 teaspoons extra virgin olive oil
* Pinch of Salt

DIRECTIONS:

1. Start by preparing the pesto:
2. After washing the zucchini, grate them, place them in a colander (to allow them to lose some excess liquid), and lightly salt them. Put the pine nuts, zucchini and basil leaves in the blender. Add the grated Parmesan, the pecorino and the extra virgin olive oil.
3. Blend everything until the mixture is creamy, stir in a pinch of salt and set aside.
4. Switch to the shrimp:
5. First of all, pull out the intestine by cutting the shrimp's back with a knife along its entire length and, with the tip of the knife, remove the black thread inside.
6. Cook the clove of garlic in a non-stick pan with extra virgin olive oil. When its browned, remove the garlic and add the shrimps. Sauté them for about 5 minutes over medium heat, until you see a crispy crust form on the outside.
7. Then, boil a pot of salted water and cook the Garganelli. Set a couple of spoons of cooking water aside,

and drain the pasta al dente.

8. Put the Garganelli in the pan where you cooked the shrimp. Cook together for a minute, add a spoon of cooking water and finally, add the zucchini pesto.

9. Mix everything well to combine the pasta with the sauce.

Nutrition (for 100g): 776 Calories 46g Fat 68g Carbohydrates 5g Protein 835mg Sodium

SALMON RISOTTO

Preparation Time : 10 minutes

Cooking Time : 30 minutes

Servings : 4

Difficulty Level : Average

INGREDIENTS:

- 1 ¾ cup (3 oz) of Rice
- 8oz Salmon steaks
- 1 Leek
- Extra virgin olive oil to taste
- 1 clove of garlic
- ½ glass white wine
- 3 ½ tablespoons grated Grana Padano
- salt to taste
- Black pepper to taste
- 17 fl. oz (500ml) Fish broth
- 1 cup butter

DIRECTIONS:

1. Start by cleaning the salmon and cutting it into small pieces. Cook 1 tablespoon of oil in a pan with a whole garlic clove and brown the salmon for 2/3 minutes, add salt and set the salmon aside, removing the garlic.

2. Now, start preparing the risotto:

3. Cut the leek into very small pieces and let it simmer in a pan over a low heat with two tablespoons of oil. Stir in the rice and cook it for a few seconds over medium-high heat, stirring with a wooden spoon.

4. Stir in the white wine and continue cooking, stirring occasionally, trying not to let the rice stick to the pan, and add the stock (vegetable or fish) gradually.

5. Halfway through cooking, add the salmon, butter, and a pinch of salt if necessary. When the rice is well cooked, remove from heat. Combine with a couple of tablespoons of grated Grana Padano and serve.

Nutrition (for 100g): 521 Calories 13g Fat 82g Carbohydrates 19g Protein 839mg Sodium

PASTA WITH CHERRY TOMATOES AND ANCHOVIES

Preparation Time : 15 minutes

Cooking Time : 35 minutes

Servings : 4

Difficulty Level : Easy

INGREDIENTS:

- 5oz Spaghetti
- 3-pound Cherry tomatoes
- 9oz Anchovies (pre-cleaned)
- 2 tablespoons Capers
- 1 clove of garlic
- 1 Small red onion
- Parsley to taste
- Extra virgin olive oil to taste
- Table salt to taste
- Black pepper to taste
- Black olives to taste

DIRECTIONS:

1. Cut the garlic clove, obtaining thin slices.
2. Cut the cherry tomatoes in Peel the onion and slice it thinly.
3. Put a little oil with the sliced garlic and onions in a saucepan. Heat everything over medium heat for 5 minutes; stir occasionally.
4. Once everything has been well flavored, add the cherry tomatoes and a pinch of salt and pepper. Cook for 15 minutes. In the meantime, situate a pot with water on the stove and as soon as it boils, add the salt and the pasta.
5. Once the sauce is almost ready, mix in the anchovies and cook for a couple of minutes. Stir gently.
6. Turn off the heat, chop the parsley and place it in the pan.
7. When its cooked, strain the pasta and stir in directly to the sauce. Turn the heat back on again for a few seconds.

Nutrition (for 100g): 446 Calories 10g Fat 1g Carbohydrates 8g Protein 934mg Sodium

BROCCOLI AND SAUSAGE ORECCHIETTE

Preparation Time : 10 minutes

Cooking Time : 32 minutes

Servings : 4

Difficulty Level : Average

INGREDIENTS:

- 5oz Orecchiette
- 5 Broccoli
- 5oz Sausage
- 35 fl. oz(40ml) White wine
- 1 clove of garlic
- 2 sprigs of thyme
- 7 teaspoons extra virgin olive oil
- Black pepper to taste
- Table salt to taste

DIRECTIONS:

1. Boil the pot with full of water and salt. Remove the broccoli florets from the stalk and cut them in half or 4 parts if they are too big; then, put them into the boiling water and cover the pot and cook for 6-7 minutes.
2. Meanwhile, finely chop thyme and set aside. Pull the gut from the sausage and with the help of a fork crush it gently.
3. Fry the garlic clove with a little olive oil and add the sausage. After a few seconds, add the thyme and a little white wine.
4. Without tossing out the cooking water, remove the cooked broccoli with the help of a slotted spoon and add them to the meat a little at a time. Cook everything for 3-4 minutes. Remove the garlic and add a pinch of black pepper.
5. Allow the water where you cooked the broccoli to reach a boil, then toss in the pasta and let it cook. Once the pasta is cooked, strain it with a slotted spoon, transferring it directly to the broccoli and sausage sauce. Then, mix well, adding black pepper and sautéing everything in the pan for a couple of minutes.

Nutrition (for 100g): 683 Calories 36g Fat 6g Carbohydrates 20g Protein 733mg Sodium

RADICCHIO AND SMOKED BACON RISOTTO

Preparation Time : 10 minutes

Cooking Time : 30 minutes

Servings : 3

Difficulty Level : Average

INGREDIENTS:

- 1 ½ cup of Rice
- 14oz Radicchio
- 3oz Smoked bacon
- 34 fl. oz (1l) Vegetable broth
- 4 fl. oz(100ml) Red wine
- 7 teaspoons extra virgin olive oil
- 7oz Shallots
- Table salt to taste
- Black pepper to taste
- 3 sprigs of thyme

DIRECTIONS:

1. Let's begin with the preparation of the vegetable broth.
2. Start with the radicchio: cut it in half and remove the central part (the white part). Cut it into strips, rinse well and set it aside. Cut the smoked bacon into tiny strips as well.
3. Finely chop the shallot and situate it in a pan with a little oil. Let it simmer over medium heat, adding a ladle of broth, then, add the bacon and let it brown.
4. After about 2 minutes, add the rice and toast it, stirring often. At this point, pour the red wine over high heat.
5. Once all the alcohol has evaporated, continue cooking adding a ladle of broth at a time. Let the previous one dry before adding another, until fully cooked. Add salt and black pepper (it's up to how much you decide to add).
6. At the end of cooking, add the strips of radicchio. Mix them well until they are blended with the rice, but without cooking them. Add the chopped thyme.

Nutrition (for 100g): 482 Calories 5g Fat 1g Carbohydrates 13g Protein 725 mg Sodium

PASTA ALA GENOVESE

Preparation Time : 10 minutes

Cooking Time : 25 minutes

Servings : 3

Difficulty Level : Average

INGREDIENTS:

- 5oz of Ziti
- 1 pound of Beef

- 2 pounds golden onions
- 2oz Celery
- 2oz Carrots
- 1 tuft of parsley
- 4 fl. oz(100ml) White wine
- Extra virgin olive oil to taste
- Table salt to taste
- Black pepper to taste
- Parmesan to taste

DIRECTIONS:

1. To prepare the pasta start by:
2. Peeling and finely chopping the onions and carrots. Then, wash and finely chop the celery (do not throw away the leaves, which must also be chopped and set aside). Next, switch to the meat, clean it of any excess fat and cut it into 5/6 large pieces. Finally, tie the celery leaves and parsley sprig with kitchen twine to create a fragrant bunch.
3. Fill plenty of oil in a large pan. Add the onions, celery, and carrots (which you had previously set aside) and let them cook for a couple of minutes.
4. Then, add the pieces of meat, a pinch of salt and the fragrant bunch. Stir and cook for a few minutes. Next, lower the heat and cover with a lid.
5. Cook for at least 3 hours (do not add water or broth because the onions will release all the liquid needed to prevent the bottom of the pan from drying). Occasionally, check on everything and stir.
6. After 3 hours of cooking, remove the bunch of herbs, increase the heat slightly, add a part of the wine and stir.
7. Cook the meat without a lid for about an hour, stirring often and adding the wine when the bottom of the pan dries.
8. At this point, take a piece of meat, cut it into slices on a cutting board and set aside. Chop the ziti and cook them in boiling salted water.
9. Once cooked, drain it and place it back in the pot. Dash a few tablespoons of cooking water and stir. Place on a plate and add a little sauce and crumbled meat (the one set aside in step 7). Add pepper and grated Parmesan to taste.

Nutrition (for 100g): 450 Calories 8g Fat 80g Carbohydrates 5g Protein 816mg Sodium

CAULIFLOWER PASTA FROM NAPLES

Preparation Time : 15 minutes

Cooking Time : 35 minutes

Servings : 3

Difficulty Level : Average

INGREDIENTS:

- 5 oz Pasta
- 1 cauliflower
- 4 fl. oz (100 ml) of tomato puree
- 1 clove of garlic
- 1 chili pepper
- 3 tablespoons extra virgin olive oil (or teaspoons)
- Salt to taste
- Pepper to taste

DIRECTIONS:

1. Clean the cauliflower well: remove the outer leaves and the stalk. Cut it into small florets.
2. Peel the garlic clove, chop it and brown it in a saucepan with the oil and the chili pepper.
3. Add the tomato puree and cauliflower florets and let them brown for a few minutes over medium heat, then cover with a few ladles of water and cook for 15-20 minutes or at least until the cauliflower begins to become creamy.
4. If you see that the bottom of the pan is too dry, add as much water as needed so that the mixture remains liquid.
5. At this point, cover the cauliflower with hot water and, once it comes to a boil, add in the pasta.
6. Season with salt and pepper.

Nutrition (for 100g): 458 Calories 18g Fat 65g Carbohydrates 9g Protein 746mg Sodium

GARLIC & TOMATO GLUTEN FREE FOCACCIA

Preparation Time : 5 minutes

Cooking Time : 20 minutes

Servings : 8

Difficulty Level : Difficult

INGREDIENTS:

- 1 egg
- ½ tsp lemon juice
- 1 tbsp honey
- 4 tbsp olive oil
- A pinch of sugar
- 1 ¼ cup warm water

- 1 tbsp active dry yeast
- 2 tsp rosemary, chopped
- 2 tsp thyme, chopped
- 2 tsp basil, chopped
- 2 cloves garlic, minced
- 1 ¼ tsp sea salt
- 2 tsp xanthan gum
- ½ cup millet flour
- 1 cup potato starch, not flour
- 1 cup sorghum flour
- Gluten free cornmeal for dusting

DIRECTIONS:

1. For 5 minutes, turn on the oven and then turn it off, while keeping oven door closed.
2. Combine warm water and pinch of sugar. Add yeast and swirl gently. Leave for 7 minutes.
3. In a large mixing bowl, whisk well herbs, garlic, salt, xanthan gum, starch, and flours. Once yeast is done proofing, pour into bowl of flours. Whisk in egg, lemon juice, honey, and olive oil.
4. Mix thoroughly and place in a well-greased square pan, dusted with cornmeal. Top with fresh garlic, more herbs, and sliced tomatoes. Place in the warmed oven and let it rise for half an hour.
5. Turn on oven to 375oF and after preheating time it for 20 minutes. Focaccia is done once tops are lightly browned. Remove from oven and pan immediately and let it cool. Best served when warm.

Nutrition (for 100g): 251 Calories 9g Fat 4g Carbohydrates 4g Protein 366mg Sodium

GRILLED BURGERS WITH MUSHROOMS

Preparation Time : 15 minutes
Cooking Time : 10 minutes
Servings : 4
Difficulty Level : Average
INGREDIENTS:

- 2 Bibb lettuce, halved
- 4 slices red onion
- 4 slices tomato
- 4 whole wheat buns, toasted
- 2 tbsp olive oil
- ¼ tsp cayenne pepper, optional
- 1 garlic clove, minced

- 1 tbsp sugar
- ½ cup water
- 1/3 cup balsamic vinegar
- 4 large Portobello mushroom caps, around 5-inches in diameter

DIRECTIONS:

1. Remove stems from mushrooms and clean with a damp cloth. Transfer into a baking dish with gill-side up.
2. In a bowl, mix thoroughly olive oil, cayenne pepper, garlic, sugar, water and vinegar. Pour over mushrooms and marinate mushrooms in the ref for at least an hour.
3. Once the one hour is nearly up, preheat grill to medium high fire and grease grill grate.
4. Grill mushrooms for five minutes per side or until tender. Baste mushrooms with marinade so it doesn't dry up.
5. To assemble, place ½ of bread bun on a plate, top with a slice of onion, mushroom, tomato and one lettuce leaf. Cover with the other top half of the bun. Repeat process with remaining ingredients, serve and enjoy.

Nutrition (for 100g): 244 Calories 3g Fat 32g Carbohydrates 1g Protein 693mg Sodium

MEDITERRANEAN COD STEW

Preparation Time : 10 minutes

Cooking Time : 20 minutes

Servings : 6

Difficulty Level : Average

INGREDIENTS:

- 2 tablespoons extra-virgin olive oil
- 2 cups chopped onion
- 2 garlic cloves, minced
- ¾ teaspoon smoked paprika
- 1 (5-ounce) can diced tomatoes, undrained
- 1 (12-ounce) jar roasted red peppers
- 1 cup sliced olives, green or black
- 1/3 cup dry red wine
- ¼ teaspoon freshly ground black pepper
- ¼ teaspoon kosher or sea salt
- 1½ pounds cod fillets, cut into 1-inch pieces
- 3 cups sliced mushrooms

DIRECTIONS:

1. Cook the oil in a stockpot. Mix in the onion and cook for 4 minutes, stirring occasionally. Stir in the garlic and smoked paprika and cook for 1 minute, stirring often.
2. Mix in the tomatoes with their juices, roasted peppers, olives, wine, pepper, and salt, and turn the heat up to medium-high. Bring to a boil. Add the cod and mushrooms, and reduce the heat to medium.
3. Cook for about 10 minutes, stir occasionally, until the cod is cooked through and flakes easily, and serve.

Nutrition (for 100g): 220 Calories 8g Fat 3g Carbohydrates 28g Protein 583mg Sodium

STEAMED MUSSELS IN WHITE WINE SAUCE

Preparation Time : 5 minutes

Cooking Time : 10 minutes

Servings : 4

Difficulty Level : Difficult

INGREDIENTS:

- 2 pounds small mussels
- 1 tablespoon extra-virgin olive oil
- 1 cup thinly sliced red onion
- 3 garlic cloves, sliced
- 1 cup dry white wine
- 2 (¼-inch-thick) lemon slices
- ¼ teaspoon freshly ground black pepper
- ¼ teaspoon kosher or sea salt
- Fresh lemon wedges, for serving (optional)

DIRECTIONS:

1. In a large colander in the sink, run cold water over the mussels (but don't let the mussels sit in standing water). All the shells should be closed tight; discard any shells that are a little bit open or any shells that are cracked. Leave the mussels in the colander until you're ready to use them.
2. In a large skillet, cook the oil. Mix in the onion and cook for 4 minutes, stirring occasionally. Place the garlic and cook for 1 minute, stirring constantly. Add the wine, lemon slices, pepper, and salt, and bring to a simmer. Cook for 2 minutes.
3. Add the mussels and cover. Cook until the mussels open their shells. Gently shake the pan two or three times while they are cooking.
4. All the shells should now be wide open. Using a slotted spoon, discard any mussels that are still closed.

Spoon the opened mussels into a shallow serving bowl, and pour the broth over the top. Serve with additional fresh lemon slices, if desired.

Nutrition (for 100g): 222 Calories 7g Fat 1g Carbohydrates 18g Protein 708mg Sodium

ORANGE AND GARLIC SHRIMP

Preparation Time : 20 minutes

Cooking Time : 10 minutes

Servings : 6

Difficulty Level : Difficult

INGREDIENTS:

- 1 large orange
- 3 tablespoons extra-virgin olive oil, divided
- 1 tablespoon chopped fresh rosemary
- 1 tablespoon chopped fresh thyme
- 3 garlic cloves, minced (about 1½ teaspoons)
- ¼ teaspoon freshly ground black pepper
- ¼ teaspoon kosher or sea salt
- 1½ pounds fresh raw shrimp, shells and tails removed

DIRECTIONS:

1. Zest the entire orange using a citrus grater. Mix the orange zest and 2 tablespoons of oil with the rosemary, thyme, garlic, pepper, and salt. Stir in the shrimp, seal the bag, and gently massage the shrimp until all the ingredients are combined and the shrimp is completely covered with the seasonings. Set aside.
2. Heat a grill, grill pan, or a large skillet over medium heat. Brush on or swirl in the remaining 1 tablespoon of oil. Add half the shrimp, and cook for 4 to 6 minutes, or until the shrimp turn pink and white, flipping halfway through if on the grill or stirring every minute if in a pan. Handover the shrimp to a large serving bowl. Repeat, and place them to the bowl.
3. While the shrimp cook, peel the orange and cut the flesh into bite-size pieces. Place to the serving bowl, and toss with the cooked shrimp. Serve immediately or refrigerate and serve cold.

Nutrition (for 100g): 190 Calories 8g Fat 1g Carbohydrates 24g Protein 647mg Sodium

ROASTED SHRIMP-GNOCCHI BAKE

Preparation Time : 10 minutes

Cooking Time : 20 minutes

Servings : 4

Difficulty Level : Average

INGREDIENTS:

- 1 cup chopped fresh tomato
- 2 tablespoons extra-virgin olive oil
- 2 garlic cloves, minced
- ½ teaspoon freshly ground black pepper
- ¼ teaspoon crushed red pepper
- 1 (12-ounce) jar roasted red peppers
- 1-pound fresh raw shrimp, shells and tails removed
- 1-pound frozen gnocchi (not thawed)
- ½ cup cubed feta cheese
- 1/3 cup fresh torn basil leaves

DIRECTIONS:

1. Preheat the oven to 425°F. In a baking dish, mix the tomatoes, oil, garlic, black pepper, and crushed red pepper. Roast in the oven for 10 minutes.

2. Stir in the roasted peppers and shrimp. Roast for 10 more minutes, until the shrimp turn pink and white.

3. While the shrimp cooks, cook the gnocchi on the stove top according to the package directions. Drain in a colander and keep warm. Remove the dish from the oven. Mix in the cooked gnocchi, feta, and basil, and serve.

Nutrition (for 100g): 277 Calories 7g Fat 1g Carbohydrates 20g Protein 711mg Sodium

SPICY SHRIMP PUTTANESCA

Preparation Time : 5 minutes

Cooking Time : 15 minutes

Servings : 4

Difficulty Level : Average

INGREDIENTS:

- 2 tablespoons extra-virgin olive oil
- 3 anchovy fillets, drained and chopped
- 3 garlic cloves, minced
- ½ teaspoon crushed red pepper
- 1 (5-ounce) can low-sodium or no-salt-added diced tomatoes, undrained
- 1 (25-ounce) can black olives
- 2 tablespoons capers
- 1 tablespoon chopped fresh oregano

- 1-pound fresh raw shrimp, shells and tails removed

DIRECTIONS:

1. Over medium heat, cook the oil. Mix in the anchovies, garlic, and crushed red pepper. Cook for 3 minutes, stirring frequently and mashing up the anchovies with a wooden spoon, until they have melted into the oil.

2. Stir in the tomatoes with their juices, olives, capers, and oregano. Turn up the heat to medium-high, and bring to a simmer.

3. When the sauce is lightly bubbling, stir in the shrimp. Select heat to medium, and cook the shrimp until they turn pink and white then serve.

Nutrition (for 100g): 214 Calories 10g Fat 2g Carbohydrates 26g Protein 591mg Sodium

ITALIAN TUNA SANDWICHES

Preparation Time : 10 minutes

Cooking Time : 0 minutes

Servings : 4

Difficulty Level : Easy

INGREDIENTS:

- 3 tablespoons freshly squeezed lemon juice
- 2 tablespoons extra-virgin olive oil
- 1 garlic clove, minced
- ½ teaspoon freshly ground black pepper
- 2 (5-ounce) cans tuna, drained
- 1 (25-ounce) can sliced olives
- ½ cup chopped fresh fennel, including fronds
- 8 slices whole-grain crusty bread

DIRECTIONS:

1. Combine the lemon juice, oil, garlic, and pepper. Add the tuna, olives, and fennel. Using a fork, separate the tuna into chunks and stir to combine all the ingredients.

2. Divide the tuna salad equally among 4 slices of bread. Top each with the remaining bread slices. Let the sandwiches sit for at least 5 minutes so the zesty filling can soak into the bread before serving.

Nutrition (for 100g): 347 Calories 17g Fat 5g Carbohydrates 25g Protein 447mg Sodium

DILL SALMON SALAD WRAPS

Preparation Time : 10 minutes

Cooking Time : 10 minutes

Servings : 6

Difficulty Level : Easy

INGREDIENTS:

- 1-pound salmon filet, cooked and flaked
- ½ cup diced carrots
- ½ cup diced celery
- 3 tablespoons chopped fresh dill
- 3 tablespoons diced red onion
- 2 tablespoons capers
- 1½ tablespoons extra-virgin olive oil
- 1 tablespoon aged balsamic vinegar
- ½ teaspoon freshly ground black pepper
- ¼ teaspoon kosher or sea salt
- 4 whole-wheat flatbread wraps or soft whole-wheat tortillas

DIRECTIONS:

1. Combine together the salmon, carrots, celery, dill, red onion, capers, oil, vinegar, pepper, and salt. Divide the salmon salad among the flatbreads. Crease the bottom of the flatbread, then roll up the wrap and serve.

Nutrition (for 100g): 336 Calories 16g Fat 5g Carbohydrates 32g Protein 884mg Sodium

WHITE CLAM PIZZA PIE

Preparation Time : 10 minutes

Cooking Time : 20 minutes

Servings : 4

Difficulty Level : Difficult

INGREDIENTS:

- 1 pound refrigerated fresh pizza dough
- Nonstick cooking spray
- 2 tablespoons extra-virgin olive oil, divided
- 2 garlic cloves, minced (about 1 teaspoon)
- ½ teaspoon crushed red pepper
- 1 (10-ounce) can whole baby clams, drained
- ¼ cup dry white wine
- All-purpose flour, for dusting
- 1 cup diced mozzarella cheese

- 1 tablespoon grated Pecorino Romano or Parmesan cheese
- 1 tablespoon chopped fresh flat-leaf (Italian) parsley

DIRECTIONS:

1. Preheat the oven to 500°F. Brush large, rimmed baking sheet with nonstick cooking spray.
2. In a large skillet, cook 1½ tablespoons of the oil. Put the garlic and crushed red pepper and cook for 1 minute, stirring frequently to prevent the garlic from burning. Add the reserved clam juice and wine. Bring to a boil over high heat. Reduce to medium heat so the sauce is just simmering and cook for 10 minutes, stirring occasionally. The sauce will cook down and thicken.
3. Place the clams and cook for 3 minutes, stirring occasionally. While the sauce is cooking, on a lightly floured surface, form the pizza dough into a 12-inch circle or into a 10-by-12-inch rectangle with a rolling pin or by stretching with your hands. Situate the dough on the prepared baking sheet. Grease the dough with the remaining ½ tablespoon of oil. Set aside until the clam sauce is ready.
4. Spread the clam sauce over the prepared dough within ½ inch of the edge. Top with the mozzarella cheese, then sprinkle with the Pecorino Romano.
5. Bake for 10 minutes. Pull out the pizza from the oven and place onto a wooden cutting board. Top with the parsley, cut into eight pieces with a pizza cutter or a sharp knife, and serve.

Nutrition (for 100g): 541 Calories 21g Fat 1g Carbohydrates 32g Protein 688mg Sodium

SLOW COOKER MEDITERRANEAN BEEF WITH ARTICHOKES

Preparation Time : 3 hours and 20 minutes
Cooking Time : 7 hours and 8 minutes
Servings : 6
Difficulty Level : Easy
INGREDIENTS:

- 2 pounds Beef for stew
- 14 ounces Artichoke hearts
- 1 tablespoon Grape seed oil
- 1 Diced onion
- 32 ounces Beef broth
- 4 cloves Garlic, grated
- 14½ ounces Tinned tomatoes, diced
- 15 ounces Tomato sauce
- 1 teaspoon Dried oregano
- ½ cup Pitted, chopped olives

- 1 teaspoon Dried parsley
- 1 teaspoon Dried oregano
- ½ teaspoon Ground cumin
- 1 teaspoon Dried basil
- 1 Bay leaf
- ½ teaspoon Salt

DIRECTIONS:

1. In a large non-stick skillet pour some oil and bring to medium-high heat. Roast the beef until it turns brown on both the sides. Transfer the beef into a slow cooker.
2. Add in beef broth, diced tomatoes, tomato sauce, salt and combine. Pour in beef broth, diced tomatoes, oregano, olives, basil, parsley, bay leaf, and cumin. Combine the mixture thoroughly.
3. Close and cook on low heat for 7 hours. Discard the bay leaf at the time serving. Serve hot.

Nutrition (for 100g): 416 Calories 5g Fat 1g Carbohydrates 9g Protein 811mg Sodium

SKINNY SLOW COOKER MEDITERRANEAN STYLE POT ROAST

Preparation Time : 30 minutes
Cooking Time : 8 hours
Servings : 10
Difficulty Level : Difficult
INGREDIENTS:

- 4 pounds Eye of round roast
- 4 cloves Garlic
- 2 teaspoons Olive oil
- 1 teaspoon Freshly ground black pepper
- 1 cup Chopped onions
- 4 Carrots, chopped
- 2 teaspoons Dried Rosemary
- 2 Chopped celery stalks
- 28 ounces Crushed tomatoes in the can
- 1 cup Low sodium beef broth
- 1 cup Red wine
- 2 teaspoons Salt

DIRECTIONS:

1. Season the beef roast with salt, garlic, and pepper and set aside. Pour oil in a non-stick skillet and bring

to medium-high heat. Put the beef into it and roast until it becomes brown on all sides. Now, transfer the roasted beef into a 6-quart slow cooker. Add carrots, onion, rosemary, and celery into the skillet. Continue cooking until the onion and vegetable become soft.

2. Stir in the tomatoes and wine into this vegetable mixture. Add beef broth and tomato mixture into the slow cooker along with the vegetable mixture. Close and cook on low for 8 hours.

3. Once the meat gets cooked, remove it from the slow cooker and place it on a cutting board and wrap with an aluminum foil. To thicken the sauce, then transfer it into a saucepan and boil it under low heat until it reaches to the required consistency. Discard fats before serving.

Nutrition (for 100g): 260 Calories 6g Fat 7g Carbohydrates 6g Protein 588mg Sodium

CHICKEN IN TOMATO-BALSAMIC PAN SAUCE

Preparation Time : 10 minutes

Cooking Time : 20 minutes

Servings : 4

Difficulty Level : Average

INGREDIENTS

- 2 (8 oz. or 7 g each) boneless chicken breasts, skinless
- ½ tsp. salt
- ½ tsp. ground pepper
- 3 tbsps. extra-virgin olive oil
- ½ c. halved cherry tomatoes
- 2 tbsps. sliced shallot
- ¼ c. balsamic vinegar
- 1 tbsp. minced garlic
- 1 tbsp. toasted fennel seeds, crushed
- 1 tbsp. butter

DIRECTIONS:

1. Slice the chicken breasts into 4 pieces and beat them with a mallet till it reaches a thickness of a ¼ inch. Use ¼ teaspoons of pepper and salt to coat the chicken. Heat two tablespoons of oil in a skillet and keep the heat to a medium. Cook the chicken breasts on both sides for three minutes. Place it to a serving plate and cover it with foil to keep it warm.

2. Add one tablespoon oil, shallot, and tomatoes in a pan and cook till it softens. Add vinegar and boil the mix till the vinegar gets reduced by half. Put fennel seeds, garlic, salt, and pepper and cook for about four minutes. Pull it out from the heat and stir it with butter. Pour this sauce over chicken and serve.

Nutrition (for 100g): 294 Calories 17g Fat 10g Carbohydrates 2g Protein 639mg Sodium

BROWN RICE, FETA, FRESH PEA, AND MINT SALAD

Preparation Time : 10 minutes

Cooking Time : 25 minutes

Servings : 4

Difficulty Level : Easy

INGREDIENTS:

- 2 c. brown rice
- 3 c. water
- Salt
- 5 oz. or 7 g crumbled feta cheese
- 2 c. cooked peas
- ½ c. chopped mint, fresh
- 2 tbsps. olive oil
- Salt and pepper

DIRECTIONS:

1. Place the brown rice, water, and salt into a saucepan over medium heat, cover, and bring to boiling point. Turn the lower heat and allow it to cook until the water has dissolved and the rice is soft but chewy. Leave to cool completely

2. Add the feta, peas, mint, olive oil, salt, and pepper to a salad bowl with the cooled rice and toss to combine Serve and enjoy!

Nutrition (for 100g): 613 Calories 2g Fat 45g Carbohydrates 12g Protein 755mg Sodium

WHOLE GRAIN PITA BREAD STUFFED WITH OLIVES AND CHICKPEAS

Preparation Time : 10 minutes

Cooking Time : 20 minutes

Servings : 2

Difficulty Level : Average

INGREDIENTS:

- 2 wholegrain pita pockets

- 2 tbsps. olive oil
- 2 garlic cloves, chopped
- 1 onion, chopped
- ½ tsp. cumin
- 10 black olives, chopped
- 2 c. cooked chickpeas
- Salt and pepper

DIRECTIONS:

1. Slice open the pita pockets and set aside Adjust your heat to medium and set a pan in place. Add in the olive oil and heat. Mix in the garlic, onion, and cumin to the hot pan and stir as the onions soften and the cumin is fragrant Add the olives, chickpeas, salt, and pepper and toss everything together until the chickpeas become golden

2. Set the pan from heat and use your wooden spoon to roughly mash the chickpeas so that some are intact and some are crushed Heat your pita pockets in the microwave, in the oven, or on a clean pan on the stove

3. Fill them with your chickpea mixture and enjoy!

Nutrition (for 100g): 503 Calories 19g Fat 14g Carbohydrates 7g Protein 798mg Sodium

ROASTED CARROTS WITH WALNUTS AND CANNELLINI BEANS

Preparation Time : 10 minutes

Cooking Time : 45 minutes

Servings : 4

Difficulty Level : Average

INGREDIENTS:

- 4 peeled carrots, chopped
- 1 c. walnuts
- 1 tbsp. honey
- 2 tbsps. olive oil
- 2 c. canned cannellini beans, drained
- 1 fresh thyme sprig
- Salt and pepper

DIRECTIONS:

1. Set oven to 400 F/204 C and line a baking tray or roasting pan with baking paper Lay the carrots and walnuts onto the lined tray or pan Sprinkle olive oil and honey over the carrots and walnuts and give

everything a rub to make sure each piece is coated Scatter the beans onto the tray and nestle into the carrots and walnuts

2. Add the thyme and sprinkle everything with salt and pepper Set tray in your oven and roast for about 40 minutes.

3. Serve and enjoy

Nutrition (for 100g): 385 Calories 27g Fat 6g Carbohydrates 18g Protein 859mg Sodium

SEASONED BUTTERED CHICKEN

Preparation Time : 10 minutes

Cooking Time : 25 minutes

Servings : 4

Difficulty Level : Average

INGREDIENTS:

- ½ c. Heavy Whipping Cream
- 1 tbsp. Salt
- ½ c. Bone Broth
- 1 tbsp. Pepper
- 4 tbsps. Butter
- 4 Chicken Breast Halves

DIRECTIONS:

1. Place cooking pan on your oven over medium heat and add in one tablespoon of butter. Once the butter is warm and melted, place the chicken in and cook for five minutes on either side. At the end of this time, the chicken should be cooked through and golden; if it is, go ahead and place it on a plate.

2. Next, you are going to add the bone broth into the warm pan. Add heavy whipping cream, salt, and pepper. Then, leave the pan alone until your sauce begins to simmer. Allow this process to happen for five minutes to let the sauce thicken up.

3. Finally, you are going to add the rest of your butter and the chicken back into the pan. Be sure to use a spoon to place the sauce over your chicken and smother it completely. Serve

Nutrition (for 100g): 350 Calories 25g Fat 10g Carbohydrates 25g Protein 869mg Sodium

DOUBLE CHEESY BACON CHICKEN

Preparation Time : 10 minutes

Cooking Time : 30 minutes

Servings : 4

Difficulty Level : Easy

INGREDIENTS:

- 4 oz. or 113 g. Cream Cheese
- 1 c. Cheddar Cheese
- 8 strips Bacon
- Sea salt
- Pepper
- 2 Garlic cloves, finely chopped
- Chicken Breast
- 1 tbsp. Bacon Grease or Butter

DIRECTIONS:

1. Ready the oven to 400 F/204 C Slice the chicken breasts in half to make them thin
2. Season with salt, pepper, and garlic Grease a baking pan with butter and place chicken breasts into it. Add the cream cheese and cheddar cheese on top of the breasts
3. Add bacon slices as well Place the pan to the oven for 30 minutes Serve hot

Nutrition (for 100g): 610 Calories 32g Fat 3g Carbohydrates 38g Protein 759mg Sodium

SHRIMPS WITH LEMON AND PEPPER

Preparation Time : 10 minutes

Cooking Time : 10 minutes

Servings : 4

Difficulty Level : Easy

INGREDIENTS:

- 40 deveined shrimps, peeled
- 6 minced garlic cloves
- Salt and black pepper
- 3 tbsps. olive oil
- ¼ tsp. sweet paprika
- A pinch crushed red pepper flake
- ¼ tsp. grated lemon zest
- 3 tbsps. Sherry or another wine
- 1½ tbsps. sliced chives
- Juice of 1 lemon

DIRECTIONS:

1. Adjust your heat to medium-high and set a pan in place.
2. Add oil and shrimp, sprinkle with pepper and salt and cook for 1 minute Add paprika, garlic and pepper

flakes, stir and cook for 1 minute. Gently stir in sherry and allow to cook for an extra minute

3. Take shrimp off the heat, add chives and lemon zest, stir and transfer shrimp to plates. Add lemon juice all over and serve

Nutrition (for 100g): 140 Calories 1g Fat 5g Carbohydrates 18g Protein 694mg Sodium

BREADED AND SPICED HALIBUT

Preparation Time : 5 minutes

Cooking Time : 25 minutes

Servings : 4

Difficulty Level : Easy

INGREDIENTS:

- ¼ c. chopped fresh chives
- ¼ c. chopped fresh dill
- ¼ tsp. ground black pepper
- ¾ c. panko breadcrumbs
- 1 tbsp. extra-virgin olive oil
- 1 tsp. finely grated lemon zest
- 1 tsp. sea salt
- 1/3 c. chopped fresh parsley
- 4 (6 oz. or 170 g. each) halibut fillets

DIRECTIONS:

1. In a medium bowl, mix olive oil and the rest ingredients except halibut fillets and breadcrumbs

2. Place halibut fillets into the mixture and marinate for 30 minutes Preheat your oven to 400 F/204 C Set a foil to a baking sheet, grease with cooking spray Dip the fillets to the breadcrumbs and put to the baking sheet Cook in the oven for 20 minutes Serve hot

Nutrition (for 100g): 667 Calories 5g Fat 2g Carbohydrates 8g Protein 756mg Sodium

CURRY SALMON WITH MUSTARD

Preparation Time : 10 minutes

Cooking Time : 20 minutes

Servings : 4

Difficulty Level : Easy

INGREDIENTS:

- ¼ tsp. ground red pepper or chili powder
- ¼ tsp. turmeric, ground

- ¼ tsp. salt
- 1 tsp. honey
- ¼ tsp. garlic powder
- 2 tsps. whole grain mustard
- 4 (6 oz. or 170 g. each) salmon fillets

DIRECTIONS:

1. In a bowl mix mustard and the rest ingredients except salmon Preheat the oven to 350 F/176 C Grease a baking dish with cooking spray. Place salmon on baking dish with skin side down and spread evenly mustard mixture on top of fillets Place into the oven and cook for 10-15 minutes or until flaky

Nutrition (for 100g): 324 Calories 9g Fat 3g Carbohydrates 34g Protein 593mg Sodium

WALNUT-ROSEMARY CRUSTED SALMON

Preparation Time : 10 minutes

Cooking Time : 25 minutes

Servings : 4

Difficulty Level : Average

INGREDIENTS:

- 1 lb. or 450 g. frozen skinless salmon fillet
- 2 tsps. Dijon mustard
- 1 clove garlic, minced
- ¼ tsp. lemon zest
- ½ tsp. honey
- ½ tsp. kosher salt
- 1 tsp. freshly chopped rosemary
- 3 tbsps. panko breadcrumbs
- ¼ tsp. crushed red pepper
- 3 tbsps. chopped walnuts
- 2 tsp. extra-virgin olive oil

DIRECTIONS:

1. Prepare the oven to 420 F/215 C and use parchment paper to line a rimmed baking sheet. In a bowl combine mustard, lemon zest, garlic, lemon juice, honey, rosemary, crushed red pepper, and salt. In another bowl mix walnut, panko, and 1 tsp oil Place parchments paper on the baking sheet and lay the salmon on it

2. Spread mustard mixture on the fish, and top with the panko mixture. Spray the rest of olive oil lightly on the salmon. Bake for about 10 -12 minutes or until the salmon is being separated by a fork Serve hot

Nutrition (for 100g): 222 Calories 12g Fat 4g Carbohydrates 8g Protein 812mg Sodium

QUICK TOMATO SPAGHETTI

Preparation Time : 10 minutes

Cooking Time : 25 minutes

Servings : 4

Difficulty Level : Average

INGREDIENTS:

- 8 oz. or 7g spaghetti
- 3 tbsps. olive oil
- 4 garlic cloves, sliced
- 1 jalapeno, sliced
- 2 c. cherry tomatoes
- Salt and pepper
- 1 tsp. balsamic vinegar
- ½ c. Parmesan, grated

DIRECTIONS:

1. Boil a large pot of water on medium flame. Add a pinch of salt and bring to a boil then add the spaghetti. Allow cooking for 8 minutes. While the pasta cooks, heat the oil in a skillet and add the garlic and jalapeno. Cook for an extra 1 minute then stir in the tomatoes, pepper, and salt.
2. Cook for 5-7 minutes until the tomatoes' skins burst.
3. Add the vinegar and remove off heat. Drain spaghetti well and mix it with the tomato sauce. Sprinkle with cheese and serve right away.

Nutrition (for 100g): 298 Calories 5g Fat 5g Carbohydrates 8g Protein 749mg Sodium

CHILI OREGANO BAKED CHEESE

Preparation Time : 10 minutes

Cooking Time : 25 minutes

Servings : 4

Difficulty Level : Easy

INGREDIENTS:

- 8 oz. or 7g feta cheese
- 4 oz. or 113g mozzarella, crumbled
- 1 sliced chili pepper
- 1 tsp. dried oregano

- 2 tbsps. olive oil

DIRECTIONS:

1. Place the feta cheese in a small deep-dish baking pan. Top with the mozzarella then season with pepper slices and oregano. cover your pan with lid. Bake in the preheated oven at 350 F/176 C for 20 minutes. Serve the cheese and enjoy it.

Nutrition (for 100g): 292 Calories 2g Fat 7g Carbohydrates 2g Protein 733mg Sodium

CRISPY ITALIAN CHICKEN

Preparation Time : 10 minutes

Cooking Time : 30 minutes

Servings : 4

Difficulty Level : Easy

INGREDIENTS:

- 4 chicken legs
- 1 tsp. dried basil
- 1 tsp. dried oregano
- Salt and pepper
- 3 tbsps. olive oil
- 1 tbsp. balsamic vinegar

DIRECTIONS:

1. Season the chicken well with basil, and oregano. Using a skillet, add oil and heat. Add the chicken in the hot oil. Let each side cook for 5 minutes until golden then cover the skillet with a lid.
2. Adjust your heat to medium and cook for 10 minutes on one side then flip the chicken repeatedly, cooking for another 10 minutes until crispy. Serve the chicken and enjoy.

Nutrition (for 100g): 262 Calories 9g Fat 11g Carbohydrates 6g Protein 693mg Sodium

SEA BASS IN A POCKET

Preparation Time : 10 minutes

Cooking Time : 25 minutes

Servings : 4

Difficulty Level : Average

INGREDIENTS:

- 4 sea bass fillets
- 4 sliced garlic cloves
- 1 sliced celery stalk

- 1 sliced zucchini
- 1 c. halved cherry tomatoes halved
- 1 shallot, sliced
- 1 tsp. dried oregano
- Salt and pepper

DIRECTIONS:

1. Mix the garlic, celery, zucchini, tomatoes, shallot, and oregano in a bowl. Add salt and pepper to taste. Take 4 sheets of baking paper and arrange them on your working surface. Spoon the vegetable mixture in the center of each sheet.

2. Top with a fish fillet then wrap the paper well so it resembles a pocket. Place the wrapped fish in a baking tray and cook in the preheated oven at 350 F/176 C for 15 minutes. Serve the fish warm and fresh.

Nutrition (for 100g): 149 Calories 8g Fat 2g Carbohydrates 2g Protein 696mg Sodium

CREAMY SMOKED SALMON PASTA

Preparation Time : 5 minutes

Cooking Time : 35 minutes

Servings : 4

Difficulty Level : Average

INGREDIENTS:

- 2 tbsps. olive oil
- 2 chopped garlic cloves
- 1 shallot, chopped
- 4 oz. or 113 g chopped salmon, smoked
- 1 c. green peas
- 1 c. heavy cream
- Salt and pepper
- 1 pinch chili flakes
- 8 oz. or 230 g penne pasta
- 6 c. water

DIRECTIONS:

1. Place skillet on medium-high heat and add oil. Add the garlic and shallot. Cook for 5 minutes or until softened. Add peas, salt, pepper, and chili flakes. Cook for 10 minutes

2. Add the salmon, and continue cooking for 5-7 minutes more. Add heavy cream, reduce heat and cook for an extra 5 minutes.

3. In the meantime, place a pan with water and salt to your taste on high heat as soon as it boils, add penne pasta and cook for 8-10 minutes or until softened Drain the pasta, add to the salmon sauce and serve

Nutrition (for 100g): 393 Calories 8g Fat 38g Carbohydrates 3g Protein 836mg Sodium

SLOW COOKER GREEK CHICKEN

Preparation Time : 20 minutes

Cooking Time : 3 hours

Servings : 4

Difficulty Level : Average

INGREDIENTS:

- 1 tablespoon extra-virgin olive oil
- 2 pounds boneless, chicken breasts
- ½ tsp kosher salt
- ¼ tsp black pepper
- 1 (12-ounce) jar roasted red peppers
- 1 cup Kalamata olives
- 1 medium red onion, cut into chunks
- 3 tablespoons red wine vinegar
- 1 tablespoon minced garlic
- 1 teaspoon honey
- 1 teaspoon dried oregano
- 1 teaspoon dried thyme
- ½ cup feta cheese (optional, for serving)
- Chopped fresh herbs: any mix of basil, parsley, or thyme (optional, for serving)

DIRECTIONS:

1. Brush slow cooker with nonstick cooking spray or olive oil. Cook the olive oil in a large skillet. Season both side of the chicken breasts. Once the oil is hot, add the chicken breasts and sear on both sides (about 3 minutes).
2. Once cooked, transfer it to the slow cooker. Add the red peppers, olives, and red onion to the chicken breasts. Try to place the vegetables around the chicken and not directly on top.
3. In a small bowl, mix the vinegar, garlic, honey, oregano, and thyme. Once combined, pour it over the chicken. Cook the chicken on low for 3 hours or until no longer pink in the middle. Serve with crumbled feta cheese and fresh herbs.

Nutrition (for 100g): 399 Calories 17g Fat 12g Carbohydrates 50g Protein 793mg Sodium

CHICKEN GYROS

Preparation Time : 10 minutes

Cooking Time : 4 hours

Servings : 4

Difficulty Level : Average

INGREDIENTS:

- 2 lbs. boneless chicken breasts or chicken tenders
- Juice of one lemon
- 3 cloves garlic
- 2 teaspoons red wine vinegar
- 2–3 tablespoons olive oil
- ½ cup Greek yogurt
- 2 teaspoons dried oregano
- 2–4 teaspoons Greek seasoning
- ½ small red onion, chopped
- 2 tablespoons dill weed
- Tzatziki Sauce
- 1 cup plain Greek yogurt
- 1 tablespoon dill weed
- 1 small English cucumber, chopped
- Pinch of salt and pepper
- 1 teaspoon onion powder
- For Toppings:
- Tomatoes
- Chopped cucumbers
- Chopped red onion
- Diced feta cheese
- Crumbled pita bread

DIRECTIONS:

1. Slice the chicken breasts into cubes and place in the slow cooker. Add the lemon juice, garlic, vinegar, olive oil, Greek yogurt, oregano, Greek seasoning, red onion, and dill to the slow cooker and stir to make sure everything is well combined.

2. Cook on low for 5–6 hours or on high for 2–3 hours. In the meantime, incorporate all ingredients for the tzatziki sauce and stir. When well mixed, put in the refrigerator until the chicken is done.

3. When the chicken has finished cooking, serve with pita bread and any or all of the toppings listed above.

Nutrition (for 100g): 317 Calories 4g Fat 1g Carbohydrates 6g Protein 476mg Sodium

CHICKPEA LETTUCE WRAPS WITH CELERY

Preparation Time : 10 minutes

Cooking Time : 0 minutes

Servings : 4

Difficulty Level : Easy

INGREDIENTS:

- 1 (15-ounce / 425-g) can low-sodium chickpeas
- 1 celery stalk, thinly sliced
- 2 tablespoons finely chopped red onion
- 2 tablespoons unsalted tahini
- 3 tablespoons honey mustard
- 1 tablespoon capers, undrained
- 12 butter lettuce leaves

DIRECTIONS:

1. In a bowl, puree the chickpeas with a potato masher or the back of a fork until mostly smooth. Add the celery, red onion, tahini, honey mustard, and capers to the bowl and stir until well incorporated.
2. For each serving, place three overlapping lettuce leaves on a plate and top with ¼ of the mashed chickpea filling, then roll up. Repeat with the remaining lettuce leaves and chickpea mixture.

Nutrition (for 100g): 182 Calories 1g Fat 3g Carbohydrates 3g Protein 743mg Sodium

GRILLED VEGETABLE SKEWERS

Preparation Time : 15 minutes

Cooking Time : 10 minutes

Servings : 4

Difficulty Level : Easy

INGREDIENTS:

- 4 medium red onions, peeled and sliced into 6 wedges
- 4 medium zucchinis, cut into 1-inch-thick slices
- 2 beefsteak tomatoes, cut into quarters
- 4 red bell peppers
- 2 orange bell peppers

- 2 yellow bell peppers
- 2 tablespoons plus 1 teaspoon olive oil

DIRECTIONS:

1. Preheat the grill to medium-high heat. Skewer the vegetables by alternating between red onion, zucchini, tomatoes, and the different colored bell peppers. Grease them with 2 tablespoons of olive oil.
2. Oil the grill grates with 1 teaspoon of olive oil and grill the vegetable skewers for 5 minutes. Flip the skewers and grill for 5 minutes more, or until they are cooked to your liking. Let the skewers cool for 5 minutes before serving.

Nutrition (for 100g): 115 Calories 3g Fat 7g Carbohydrates 5g Protein 647mg Sodium

STUFFED PORTOBELLO MUSHROOM WITH TOMATOES

Preparation Time : 10 minutes

Cooking Time : 15 minutes

Servings : 4

Difficulty Level : Average

INGREDIENTS:

- 4 large portobello mushroom caps
- 3 tablespoons extra-virgin olive oil
- Salt and black pepper, to taste
- 4 sun-dried tomatoes
- 1 cup shredded mozzarella cheese, divided
- ½ to ¾ cup low-sodium tomato sauce

DIRECTIONS:

1. Preheat the broiler on high. Lay the mushroom caps on a baking sheet and drizzle with olive oil. Sprinkle with salt and pepper. Broil for 1o minutes, flipping the mushroom caps halfway through, until browned on the top.
2. Remove from the broil. Spoon 1 tomato, 2 tablespoons of cheese, and 2 to 3 tablespoons of sauce onto each mushroom cap. Return the mushroom caps to the broiler and continue broiling for 2 to 3 minutes. Cool for 5 minutes before serving.

Nutrition (for 100g): 217 Calories 8g Fat 9g Carbohydrates 2g Protein 793mg Sodium

EGG CASSEROLE WITH PAPRIKA

Preparation Time : 10 minutes

Cooking Time : 28 minutes

Servings : 4

Difficulty Level : Average

INGREDIENTS:

- 2 eggs, beaten
- 1 red bell pepper, chopped
- 1 chili pepper, chopped
- ½ red onion, diced
- 1 teaspoon canola oil
- ½ teaspoon salt
- 1 teaspoon paprika
- 1 tablespoon fresh cilantro, chopped
- 1 garlic clove, diced
- 1 teaspoon butter, softened
- ¼ teaspoon chili flakes

DIRECTIONS:

1. Brush the casserole mold with canola oil and pour beaten eggs inside. After this, toss the butter in the skillet and melt it over the medium heat. Add chili pepper and red bell pepper.
2. After this, add red onion and cook the vegetables for 7-8 minutes over the medium heat. Stir them from time to time. Transfer the vegetables in the casserole mold.
3. Add salt, paprika, cilantro, diced garlic, and chili flakes. Stir mildly with the help of a spatula to get a homogenous mixture. Bake the casserole for 20 minutes at 355F in the oven. Then chill the meal well and cut into servings. Transfer the casserole in the serving plates with the help of the spatula.

Nutrition (for 100g): 68 Calories 5g Fat 1g Carbohydrates 4g Protein 882mg Sodium

CAULIFLOWER FRITTERS

Preparation Time : 10 minutes

Cooking Time : 10 minutes

Servings : 2

Difficulty Level : Easy

INGREDIENTS :

- 1 cup cauliflower, shredded
- 1 egg, beaten
- 1 tablespoon wheat flour, whole grain
- 1 oz Parmesan, grated

- ½ teaspoon ground black pepper
- 1 tablespoon canola oil

DIRECTIONS:

1. In the mixing bowl mix up together shredded cauliflower and egg. Add wheat flour, grated Parmesan, and ground black pepper. Stir the mixture with the help of the fork until it is homogenous and smooth.
2. Pour canola oil in the skillet and bring it to boil. Make the fritters from the cauliflower mixture with the help of the fingertips or use spoon and transfer in the hot oil. Roast the fritters for 4 minutes from each side over the medium-low heat.

Nutrition (for 100g): 167 Calories 3g Fat 5g Carbohydrates 8g Protein 705mg Sodium

CREAMY OATMEAL WITH FIGS

Preparation Time : 10 minutes
Cooking Time : 20 minutes
Servings : 5
Difficulty Level : Easy
INGREDIENTS:

- 2 cups oatmeal
- 1 ½ cup milk
- 1 tablespoon butter
- 3 figs, chopped
- 1 tablespoon honey

DIRECTIONS:

1. Pour milk in the saucepan. Add oatmeal and close the lid. Cook the oatmeal for 15 minutes over the medium-low heat. Then add chopped figs and honey.
2. Add butter and mix up the oatmeal well. Cook it for 5 minutes more. Close the lid and let the cooked breakfast rest for 10 minutes before serving.

Nutrition (for 100g): 222 Calories 6g Fat 4g Carbohydrates 1g Protein 822mg Sodium

BAKED OATMEAL WITH CINNAMON

Preparation Time : 10 minutes
Cooking Time : 25 minutes
Servings : 4
Difficulty Level : Easy
INGREDIENTS:

- 1 cup oatmeal

- 1/3 cup milk
- 1 pear, chopped
- 1 teaspoon vanilla extract
- 1 tablespoon Splenda
- 1 teaspoon butter
- ½ teaspoon ground cinnamon
- 1 egg, beaten

DIRECTIONS:

1. In the big bowl mix up together oatmeal, milk, egg, vanilla extract, Splenda, and ground cinnamon. Melt butter and add it in the oatmeal mixture. Then add chopped pear and stir it well.
2. Transfer the oatmeal mixture in the casserole mold and flatten gently. Cover it with the foil and secure edges. Bake the oatmeal for 25 minutes at 350F.

Nutrition (for 100g): 151 Calories 9g Fat 3g Carbohydrates 9g Protein 753mg Sodium

ALMOND CHIA PORRIDGE

Preparation Time : 10 minutes
Cooking Time : 30 minutes
Servings : 4
Difficulty Level : Easy
INGREDIENTS:

- 3 cups organic almond milk
- 1/3 cup chia seeds, dried
- 1 teaspoon vanilla extract
- 1 tablespoon honey
- ¼ teaspoon ground cardamom

DIRECTIONS:

1. Pour almond milk in the saucepan and bring it to boil. Then chill the almond milk to the room temperature (or appx. For 10-15 minutes). Add vanilla extract, honey, and ground cardamom. Stir well. After this, add chia seeds and stir again. Close the lid and let chia seeds soak the liquid for 20-25 minutes. Transfer the cooked porridge into the serving ramekins.

Nutrition (for 100g): 150 Calories 3g Fat 1g Carbohydrates 7g Protein 836mg Sodium

COCOA OATMEAL

Preparation Time : 10 minutes
Cooking Time : 15 minutes

Servings : 2

Difficulty Level : Easy

INGREDIENTS:

- 1 ½ cup oatmeal
- 1 tablespoon cocoa powder
- ½ cup heavy cream
- ¼ cup of water
- 1 teaspoon vanilla extract
- 1 tablespoon butter
- 2 tablespoons Splenda

DIRECTIONS :

1. Mix up together oatmeal with cocoa powder and Splenda. Transfer the mixture in the saucepan. Add vanilla extract, water, and heavy cream. Stir it gently with the help of the spatula.

2. Close the lid and cook it for 10-15 minutes over the medium-low heat. Remove the cooked cocoa oatmeal from the heat and add butter. Stir it well.

Nutrition (for 100g): 230 Calories 6g Fat 5g Carbohydrates 6g Protein 691mg Sodium

CINNAMON ROLL OATS

Preparation Time : 7 minutes

Cooking Time : 10 minutes

Servings : 4

Difficulty Level : Easy

INGREDIENTS:

- ½ cup rolled oats
- 1 cup milk
- 1 teaspoon vanilla extract
- 1 teaspoon ground cinnamon
- 2 teaspoon honey
- 2 tablespoons Plain yogurt
- 1 teaspoon butter

DIRECTIONS:

1. Transfer milk in the saucepan and bring it to boil. Add rolled oats and stir well. Close the lid and simmer the oats for 5 minutes over the medium heat. The cooked oats will absorb all milk.

2. Then add butter and stir the oats well. In the separated bowl, whisk together Plain yogurt with honey, cinnamon, and vanilla extract. Transfer the cooked oats in the serving bowls. Top the oats with the

yogurt mixture in the shape of the wheel.

Nutrition (for 100g): 243 Calories 2g Fat 1g Carbohydrates 3g Protein 697mg Sodium

PUMPKIN OATMEAL WITH SPICES

Preparation Time : 10 minutes

Cooking Time : 13 minutes

Servings : 6

Difficulty Level : Easy

INGREDIENTS :

- 2 cups oatmeal
- 1 cup of coconut milk
- 1 cup milk
- 1 teaspoon Pumpkin pie spices
- 2 tablespoons pumpkin puree
- 1 tablespoon Honey
- ½ teaspoon butter

DIRECTIONS:

1. Pour coconut milk and milk in the saucepan. Add butter and bring the liquid to boil. Add oatmeal, stir well with the help of a spoon and close the lid.
2. Simmer the oatmeal for 7 minutes over the medium heat. Meanwhile, mix up together honey, pumpkin pie spices, and pumpkin puree. When the oatmeal is cooked, add pumpkin puree mixture and stir well. Transfer the cooked breakfast in the serving plates.
3. **Nutrition (for 100g):** 232 Calories 5g Fat 8g Carbohydrates 9g Protein 708mg Sodium

STEWED CINNAMON APPLES WITH DATES

Preparation Time : 15 minutes

Cooking Time : 10 minutes

Servings : 6

Difficulty Level : Easy

INGREDIENTS:

- 4 large Pink Lady apples
- ½ cup water
- ¼ cup chopped pitted dates

- 1 teaspoon ground cinnamon
- ¼ teaspoon vanilla extract
- 1 teaspoon unsalted butter

DIRECTIONS:

1. Place apples, water, dates, and cinnamon in the Instant Pot. Close, let steam release, press the Manual button, and set the timer to 3 minutes.
2. When the alarm beeps, quick-release the pressure until the float valve sets. Click the Cancel button and open lid. Stir in vanilla and butter. Serve hot or chilled.

Nutrition (for 100g): 111 Calories 2g Fat 6g Carbohydrates 1g Protein 411mg Sodium

SPICED POACHED PEARS

Preparation Time : 10 minutes

Cooking Time : 15 minutes

Servings : 4

Difficulty Level : Easy

INGREDIENTS:

- 2 cups water
- 2 cups red wine
- ¼ cup honey
- 4 whole cloves
- 2 cinnamon sticks
- 1-star anise
- 1 teaspoon vanilla bean paste
- 4 Bartlett pears, peeled

DIRECTIONS:

1. Place all elements in the Instant Pot and mix. Cover, set steam release to Sealing, press the Manual Instant Pot. Stir to couple. Close lid, let steam release to Seal click the Manual button, and alarm to 3 minutes.
2. When the timer beeps, swiftly-release the pressure until the float valve drops. Select the Cancel and open. Take out pears to a plate and allow to cool for 5 minutes. Serve warm.

Nutrition (for 100g): 194 Calories 5g Fat 4g Carbohydrates 1g Protein 366mg Sodium

CRANBERRY APPLESAUCE

Preparation Time : 10 minutes

Cooking Time : 20 minutes

Servings : 8

Difficulty Level : Easy

INGREDIENTS:

- 1 cup whole cranberries
- 4 medium tart apples, peeled, cored, and grated
- 4 medium sweet apples, peeled, cored, and grated
- 1½ tablespoons grated orange zest
- ¼ cup orange juice
- ¼ cup dark brown sugar
- ¼ cup granulated sugar
- 1 tablespoon unsalted butter
- 2 teaspoons ground cinnamon
- ½ teaspoon ground cloves
- ¼ teaspoon ground black pepper
- 1/8 teaspoon salt
- 1 tablespoon lemon juice

DIRECTIONS:

1. Incorporate all ingredients in the Instant Pot. Seal then, set the Manual button, and time to 5 minutes. When the timer beeps, let pressure release naturally, about 25 minutes. Open the lid. Lightly mash fruit with a fork. Stir well. Serve warm or cold.

Nutrition (for 100g): 136 Calories 4g Fat 3g Carbohydrates 9g Protein 299mg Sodium

SPANISH CRUMBLE CAKES

Preparation Time : 10 minutes

Cooking Time : 25 minutes

Servings : 30

Difficulty Level : Difficult

INGREDIENTS:

- 2 cups flour
- 1 cup butter, softened
- 1 cup sugar
- 1 egg
- 1 tsp lemon zest
- 1 tsp orange zest
- 1 tbsp orange juice

- 1/2 cup almonds, blanched and finely ground

DIRECTIONS:

1. Beat butter with sugar, lemon and orange zest until light. Combine in the flour, using a wooden spoon. Add ground almonds, stir, then knead with your hands until dough clings together. Divide it in three parts. Seal and chill for at least half an hour.
2. On a well-floured surface, roll out each piece of dough until it is 1/4 inch thick. Cut into different shapes. Arrange cookies on an ungreased baking sheet.
3. Beat together egg and orange juice and brush this over the cookies. Bake in a preheated to 350 degrees F oven for 7-8 minutes, or until edges are lightly golden. Set aside and keep in an airtight container.

Nutrition (for 100g): 113 Calories 8g Fats 5g Carbohydrates 4g Protein 204mg Sodium

GREEK HONEY COOKIES

Preparation Time : 10 minutes

Cooking Time : 15 minutes

Servings : 40

Difficulty Level : Difficult

INGREDIENTS:

- 1 ¾ cups olive oil
- 2 cups walnuts, coarsely ground
- 1 cup sugar
- 1 cup fresh orange juice
- 3 tbsp orange peel
- 1/3 cup cognac
- 1 ½ tsp baking soda
- 1 tsp baking powder
- sifted flour, enough to make soft oily dough
- for the syrup
- 2 cups honey
- 1 cup water
- for sprinkling
- 1 cup very finely ground walnuts
- 1 tsp ground cinnamon
- 1 tsp ground cloves

DIRECTIONS:

1. Line 2 baking trays with baking paper. In a very large bowl, scourge together oil, sugar, orange zest,

orange juice, cognac, baking soda, baking powder, and salt until well combined. Fold in flour with a wooden spoon until a soft dough is formed.

2. Roll tablespoonfuls of the mixture into balls. Place them, about 5 inch apart, on the prepared trays. With a fork to prick the top of each cookie by cross-pressing. Bake in a preheated to 350 degrees F oven, for 30-35 minutes, or until golden.

3. Situate the water and honey in a medium saucepan over medium-high heat. Simmer for 5 minutes, removing foam. Lower heat and with the help of a perforated spoon, dip 5-6 cookies at a time into the syrup. Once the cookies have absorbed a little of the syrup, remove them with the same spoon and situate them on a tray to cool and get rid of any excess syrup. After dipping the cookies, sprinkle with a mixture of cinnamon, cloves and finely ground walnuts.

Nutrition (for 100g): 116 Calories 7g Fats 6g Carbohydrates 2g Protein 241mg Sodium

CINNAMON BUTTER COOKIES

Preparation Time : 10 minutes

Cooking Time : 20 minutes

Servings : 24

Difficulty Level : Average

INGREDIENTS:

- 2 cups flour
- 1/2 cup sugar
- 5 tbsp butter
- 3 eggs
- 1 tbsp cinnamon

DIRECTIONS:

1. Scourge the butter and sugar until light and fluffy. Combine the flour and the cinnamon. Beat eggs into the butter mixture. Gently add in the flour. Situate the dough onto a lightly floured surface and knead just once or twice until smooth.

2. Form a roll and divide it into 24 pieces. Grease and line baking sheets with parchment paper. Spread each piece of cookie dough into a long thin strip, then make a circle, flatten a little and set it on the prepared baking sheet. Bake cookies, in batches, in a preheated to 350 F oven, for 12 to 15 minutes. Set aside in a cooling rack.

Nutrition (for 100g): 111 Calories 5g Fats 3g Carbohydrates 9g Protein 230mg Sodium

BEST FRENCH MERINGUES

Preparation Time : 10 minutes

Cooking Time : 2 hours and 30 minutes

Servings : 36

Difficulty Level : Average

INGREDIENTS:

- 4 egg whites
- 2 1/4 cups powdered sugar

DIRECTIONS:

1. Ready the oven to 200 F and line a baking sheet.
2. In a glass bowl, beat egg whites with an electric mixer. Mix in sugar a little simultaneously, while continuing to beat at medium speed. When the egg white mixture becomes stiff and shiny like satin, transfer to a large pastry bag. Place the meringue onto the lined baking sheet with the use of a large round.
3. Put the meringues in the oven and leave the oven door slightly ajar. Bake until the meringues are dry.

Nutrition (for 100g): 110 Calories 11g Fat 6g Carbohydrates 3g Protein 230mg Sodium

CINNAMON PALMIER

Preparation Time : 5 minutes

Cooking Time : 15 minutes

Servings : 30

Difficulty Level : Easy

INGREDIENTS:

- 1/3 cup granulated sugar
- 2 tsp cinnamon
- 1/2 lb. puff pastry
- 1 egg, beaten (optional)

DIRECTIONS:

1. Stir together the sugar and cinnamon. Spread the pastry dough into a large rectangle. Spread the cinnamon sugar in an even layer over the dough. From the long ends of the rectangle, loosely roll each side inward until they meet in the middle. If needed, brush it with the egg to hold it together. Slice the pastry roll crosswise into 1/4-inch pieces and arrange them on a lined with parchment paper baking sheet. Bake cookies in a preheated to 400 F oven for 12-15 minutes, until they puff and turn golden brown. Serve warm or at room temperature.

Nutrition (for 100g): 114 Calories 3g Fats 8g Carbohydrates 6g Protein 274mg Sodium

HONEY SESAME COOKIES

Preparation Time : 10 minutes

Cooking Time : 15 minutes

Servings : 30

Difficulty Level : Difficult

INGREDIENTS:

- 3 cups flour
- 1 cup sugar
- 1 cup butter
- 2 eggs
- 3 tbsp honey
- 1 cup pistachio nuts, roughly chopped
- 1 cup sesame seeds
- 1 tbsp vinegar
- 1 tsp vanilla
- 1 tsp baking powder
- a pinch of salt

DIRECTIONS:

1. Scourge the butter and the sugar until light and fluffy. Gently add in the eggs, then the vanilla extract and the vinegar. Incorporate the flour, salt, and baking powder and stir in the butter mixture. Beat until just incorporated. Cover and refrigerate for an hour.
2. Mix the sesame seeds and the honey in a medium plate. Place the pistachios in another one. Take a teaspoonful of dough, form it into a ball, then dip it into the pistachios. Press a little and dip it into the sesame-honey mixture. Repeat with the remaining dough, arranging the cookies on a lined baking sheet.
3. Bake the cookies in a preheated to 350 F oven for 15 minutes, or until they turn light brown. Set aside in the baking sheet for 2-3 minutes then move to a wire rack.

Nutrition (for 100g): 117 Calories 9g Fats 7g Carbohydrates 1g Protein 214mg Sodium

BAKED APPLES

Preparation Time : 5 minutes

Cooking Time : 10 minutes

Servings : 4

Difficulty Level : Easy

INGREDIENTS:

- 8 medium sized apples
- 1/3 cup walnuts, crushed

- 3/4 cup sugar
- 3 tbsp raisins, soaked in brandy or dark rum
- vanilla, cinnamon according to taste
- 2 oz butter

DIRECTIONS:

1. Peel and carefully hollow the apples. Prepare stuffing by beating the butter, 3/4 cup of sugar, crushed walnuts, raisins and cinnamon. Fill in the apples with this mixture and situate them in an oiled dish. Sprinkle the apples with 1-2 tablespoons of water and bake in a moderate oven. Serve warm and side it with vanilla ice cream.

Nutrition (for 100g): 107 Calories 9g Fats 7g Carbohydrates 3g Protein 236mg Sodium

PUMPKIN BAKED WITH DRY FRUIT

Preparation Time : 10 minutes
Cooking Time : 15 minutes
Servings : 6
Difficulty Level : Easy
INGREDIENTS:

- 5 lb. pumpkin, cut into medium pieces
- 1 cup dry fruit (apricots, plums, apples, raisins)
- 1/2 cup brown sugar

DIRECTIONS:

1. Soak the dry fruit in some water, drain and discard the water. Cut the pumpkin in medium cubes. At the bottom of a pot arrange a layer of pumpkin pieces, then a layer of dry fruit and then again, some pumpkin. Add a little water. Cover the pot and bring to boil. Simmer until there is no more water. When almost ready add the sugar. Serve warm or cold.

Nutrition (for 100g): 113 Calories 8g Fats 5g Carbohydrates 3g Protein 311mg Sodium

BANANA SHAKE BOWLS

Preparation Time : 5 minutes
Cooking Time : 0 minutes
Servings : 4
Difficulty Level : Easy
INGREDIENTS:

- 4 medium bananas, peeled
- 1 avocado, peeled, pitted and mashed

- ¾ cup almond milk
- ½ teaspoon vanilla extract

DIRECTIONS:

1. In a blender, meld the bananas with the avocado and the other ingredients, pulse, divide into bowls and store in the fridge until serving.

Nutrition (for 100g): 185 Calories 3g Fat 6g Carbohydrates 45g Protein 214mg Sodium

COLD LEMON SQUARES

Preparation Time : 30 minutes

Cooking Time : 0 minutes

Servings : 4

Difficulty Level : Easy

INGREDIENTS:

- 1 cup avocado oil+ a drizzle
- 2 bananas, peeled and chopped
- 1 tablespoon honey
- ¼ cup lemon juice
- A pinch of lemon zest, grated

DIRECTIONS:

1. In your food processor, mix the bananas with the rest of the ingredients, pulse well and spread on the bottom of a pan greased with a drizzle of oil. Introduce in the fridge for 30 minutes, slice into squares and serve.

Nutrition (for 100g): 136 Calories 2g Fat 7g Carbohydrates 1g Protein 236mg Sodium

BLACKBERRY AND APPLES COBBLER

Preparation Time : 10 minutes

Cooking Time : 30 minutes

Servings : 6

Difficulty Level : Average

INGREDIENTS:

- ¾ cup stevia
- 6 cups blackberries
- ¼ cup apples, cored and cubed
- ¼ teaspoon baking powder
- 1 tablespoon lime juice

- ½ cup almond flour
- ½ cup water
- 3 and ½ tablespoon avocado oil
- Cooking spray

DIRECTIONS:

1. In a bowl, combine the berries with half of the stevia and lemon juice, sprinkle some flour all over, whisk and pour into a baking dish greased with cooking spray.
2. In another bowl, mix flour with the rest of the sugar, baking powder, the water and the oil, and stir the whole thing with your hands. Spread over the berries, introduce in the oven at 375 degrees F and bake for 30 minutes.
3. Serve warm.

Nutrition (for 100g): 221 Calories 3g Fat 6g Carbohydrates 9g Protein 350mg Sodium

BLACK TEA CAKE

Preparation Time : 10 minutes

Cooking Time : 35 minutes

Servings : 8

Difficulty Level : Average

INGREDIENTS:

- 6 tablespoons black tea powder
- 2 cups almond milk, warmed up
- 1 cup avocado oil
- 2 cups stevia
- 4 eggs
- 2 teaspoons vanilla extract
- 3 and ½ cups almond flour
- 1 teaspoon baking soda
- 3 teaspoons baking powder

DIRECTIONS:

1. Stir well the almond milk with the oil, stevia and the rest of the ingredients. Pour this into a cake pan lined with parchment paper, introduce in the oven at 350 degrees F and bake for 35 minutes. Leave the cake to cool down, slice and serve.

Nutrition (for 100g): 200 Calories 4g Fat 5g Carbohydrates 4g Protein 384mg Sodium

GREEN TEA AND VANILLA CREAM

Preparation Time : 2 hours

Cooking Time : 0 minutes

Servings : 4

Difficulty Level : Easy

INGREDIENTS:

- 14 ounces almond milk, hot
- 2 tablespoons green tea powder
- 14 ounces heavy cream
- 3 tablespoons stevia
- 1 teaspoon vanilla extract
- 1 teaspoon gelatin powder

DIRECTIONS:

1. Incorporate well the almond milk with the green tea powder and the rest of the ingredients, cool down, divide into cups and keep in the fridge for 2 hours before serving.

Nutrition (for 100g): 120 Calories 3g Fat 7g Carbohydrates 4g Protein 293mg Sodium

PEACH BREAKFAST SALAD

Preparation Time : 10 minutes

Cooking Time : 0 minutes

Servings : 1

Difficulty Level : Easy

INGREDIENTS:

- 1/4 Cup Walnuts, Chopped & Toasted
- 1 Teaspoon Honey, Raw
- 1 Peach, Pitted & Sliced
- 1/2 Cup Cottage Cheese, Nonfat & Room Temperature
- 1 Tablespoon Mint, Fresh & Chopped
- 1 Lemon, Zested

DIRECTIONS:

1. Place your cottage cheese in a bowl, and top with peach slices and walnuts. Drizzle with honey, and top with mint.
2. Sprinkle on your lemon zest before serving immediately.

Nutrition (for 100g): 280 calories 11g fats 19g carbohydrates 39g protein 527mg sodium

SAVORY OATS

Preparation Time : 10 minutes

Cooking Time : 10 minutes

Servings : 2

Difficulty Level : Easy

INGREDIENTS:

- 1/2 Cup Steel Cut Oats

- 1 Cup Water

- 1 Tomato, Large & Chopped

- 1 Cucumber, Chopped

- 1 Tablespoon Olive Oil

- Sea Salt & Black Pepper to Taste

- Flat Leaf Parsley, Chopped to Garnish

- Parmesan Cheese, Low Fat & Freshly Grated

DIRECTIONS:

1. Bring your oats and a cup of water to a boil using a saucepan over high heat. Stir often until your water is completely absorbed, which will take roughly fifteen minutes. Divide between two bowls, and top with tomatoes and cucumber. Drizzle with olive oil and top with parmesan. Garnish with parsley before serving.

Nutrition (for 100g): 408 calories 13g fats 10g carbohydrates 28g protein 825mg sodium

TAHINI & APPLE TOAST

Preparation Time : 15 minutes

Cooking Time : 0 minutes

Servings : 1

Difficulty Level : Easy

INGREDIENTS:

- 2 Tablespoons Tahini

- 2 Slices Whole Wheat Bread, Toasted

- 1 Teaspoon Honey, Raw

- 1 Apple, Small, Cored & Sliced Thin

DIRECTIONS:

1. Start by spreading the tahini over your toast, and then lay your apples over it. drizzle with honey before serving.

Nutrition (for 100g): 366 calories 13g fats 9g carbohydrates 29g protein 686mg sodium

SCRAMBLED BASIL EGGS

Preparation Time : 5 minutes

Cooking Time : 10 minutes

Servings : 2

Difficulty Level : Easy

INGREDIENTS:

- 4 Eggs, Large
- 2 Tablespoons Fresh Basil, Chopped Fine
- 2 Tablespoons Gruyere Cheese, Grated
- 1 Tablespoon Cream
- 1 Tablespoon Olive Oil
- 2 Cloves Garlic, Minced
- Sea Salt & Black Pepper to Taste

DIRECTIONS:

1. Get out a large bowl and beat your basil, cheese, cream and eggs together. Whisk until it's well combined. Get out a large skillet over medium-low heat, and heat your oil. Add in your garlic, cooking for a minute. It should turn golden.
2. Pour the egg mixture into your skillet over the garlic, and then continue to scramble as they cook so they become soft and fluffy. Season it well and serve warm.

Nutrition (for 100g): 360 calories 14g fats 8g carbohydrates 29g protein 545mg sodium

GREEK POTATOES & EGGS

Preparation Time : 10 minutes

Cooking Time : 30 minutes

Servings : 2

Difficulty Level : Easy

INGREDIENTS:

- 3 tomatoes, seeded & roughly chopped
- 2 tablespoons basil, fresh & chopped
- 1 clove garlic, minced
- 2 tablespoons + ½ cup olive oil, divided
- sea salt & black pepper to taste
- 3 russet potatoes, large
- 4 eggs, large

- 1 teaspoon oregano, fresh & chopped

DIRECTIONS:

1. Get the food processor and place your tomatoes in, pureeing them with the skin on.
2. Add your garlic, two tablespoons of oil, salt, pepper and basil. Pulse until it's well combined. Place this mixture in a skillet, cooking while covered for twenty to twenty-five minutes over low heat. Your sauce should be thickened as well as bubbly.
3. Dice your potatoes into cubes, and then place them in a skillet with a ½ a cup of olive oil in a skillet using medium-low heat.
4. Fry your potatoes until crisp and browned. This should take five minutes, and then cover the skillet, reducing the heat to low. Steam them until your potatoes are done.
5. Stir in the eggs into the tomato sauce, and cook using low heat for six minutes. Your eggs should be set.
6. Remove the potatoes from your pan, and drain using paper towels. Place them in a bowl. Sprinkle in your salt, pepper and oregano, and then serve your eggs with potatoes. Drizzle your sauce over the mixture, and serve warm.

Nutrition (for 100g): 348 calories 12g fats 7g carbohydrates 27g protein 469mg sodium

AVOCADO & HONEY SMOOTHIE

Preparation Time : 5 minutes

Cooking Time : 0 minutes

Servings : 2

Difficulty Level : Easy

INGREDIENTS:

- 1 1/2 cups soy milk
- 1 avocado, large
- 2 tablespoons honey, raw

DIRECTIONS:

1. Incorporate all ingredients together and blend until smooth, and serve immediately.

Nutrition (for 100g): 280 calories 19g fats 11g carbohydrates 30g protein 547mg sodium

VEGETABLE FRITTATA

Preparation Time : 5 minutes

Cooking Time : 10 minutes

Servings : 2

Difficulty Level : Easy

INGREDIENTS:

- 1/2 baby eggplant, peeled & diced
- 1 handful baby spinach leaves
- 1 tablespoon olive oil
- 3 eggs, large
- 1 teaspoon almond milk
- 1-ounce goat cheese, crumbled
- 1/4 small red pepper, chopped
- sea salt & black pepper to taste

DIRECTIONS:

1. Start by heating the broiler on your oven, and then beat the eggs together with almond milk. Make sure it's well combined, and then get out a nonstick, oven proof skillet. Place it over medium-high heat, and then add in your olive oil.
2. Once your oil is heated, add in your eggs. Spread your spinach over this mixture in an even layer, and top with the rest of your vegetables.
3. Reduce your heat to medium, and sprinkle with salt and pepper. Allow your vegetables and eggs to cook for five minutes. The bottom half of your eggs should be firm, and your vegetables should be tender. Top with goat cheese, and then broil on the middle rack for three to five minutes. Your eggs should be all the way done, and your cheese should be melted. Slice into wedges and serve warm.

Nutrition (for 100g): 340 calories 16g fats 9g carbohydrates 37g protein 748mg sodium

MINI LETTUCE WRAPS

Preparation Time : 15 minutes
Cooking Time : 0 minutes
Servings : 4
Difficulty Level : Easy
INGREDIENTS:

- 1 cucumber, diced
- 1 red onion, sliced
- 1-ounce feta cheese, low fat & crumbed
- 1 lemon, juiced
- 1 tomato, diced
- 1 tablespoon olive oil
- 12 small iceberg lettuce leaves
- sea salt & black pepper to taste

DIRECTIONS:

1. Combine your tomato, onion, feta, and cucumber in a bowl. Mix your oil and juice, and season with salt and pepper.
2. Fill each leaf with the vegetable mixture, and roll them tightly. Use a toothpick to keep them together to serve.

Nutrition (for 100g): 291 calories 10g fats 9g carbohydrates 27g protein 655mg sodium

CURRY APPLE COUSCOUS

Preparation Time : 20 minutes

Cooking Time : 5 minutes

Servings : 4

Difficulty Level : Average

INGREDIENTS:

- 2 teaspoons olive oil
- 2 leeks, white parts only, sliced
- 1 apple, diced
- 2 tablespoons curry powder
- 2 cups couscous, cooked & whole wheat
- 1/2 cup pecans, chopped

DIRECTIONS:

1. Heat your oil in a skillet using medium heat. Add the leeks, and cook until tender, which will take five minutes. Add in your apple, and cook until soft.
2. Add in your curry powder and couscous, and stir well. Remove from heat, and mix in your nuts before serving immediately.

Nutrition (for 100g): 330 calories 12g fats 8g carbohydrates 30g protein 824mg sodium

LAMB & VEGETABLE BAKE

Preparation Time : 20 minutes

Cooking Time : 1 hour and 10 minutes

Servings : 8

Difficulty Level : Average

INGREDIENTS:

- 1/4 cup olive oil
- 1 lb. lean lamb, boneless & chopped into ½ inch pieces
- 2 red potatoes, large, scrubbed & diced
- 1 onion, chopped roughly
- 2 cloves garlic, minced
- 28 ounces diced tomatoes with liquid, canned & no salt
- 2 zucchinis, cut into ½ inch slices
- 1 red bell pepper, seeded & cut into 1-inch cubes
- 2 tablespoons flat leaf parsley, chopped

- 1 tablespoon paprika
- 1 teaspoon thyme
- 1/2 teaspoon cinnamon
- 1/2 cup red wine
- sea salt & black pepper to taste

DIRECTIONS:

1. Start by turning the oven to 325, and then get out a large stew pot. Place it over medium-high heat to heat your olive oil. Once your oil is hot stir in your lamb, browning the meat. Stir frequently to keep it from running, and then place your lamb in a baking dish. Cook your garlic, onion and potatoes in the skillet until they're tender, which should take five to six minutes more. Place them to the baking dish as well. Pour the zucchini, pepper, and tomatoes in the pan with your herbs and spices. Allow it to simmer for ten minutes more before pouring it into your baking dish. Pour in the wine and pepper sauce. Add in your tomato, and then cover with foil. Bake for an hour. Take the cover off for the last fifteen minutes of baking, and adjust seasoning as needed.

Nutrition (for 100g): 240 calories 14g fats 8g carbohydrates 36g protein 427mg sodium

HERB FLOUNDER

Preparation Time : 20 minutes
Cooking Time : 1 hour and 5 minutes
Servings : 4
Difficulty Level : Average
INGREDIENTS:

- 1/2 cup flatleaf parsley, lightly packed
- 1/4 cup olive oil
- 4 cloves garlic, peeled & halved
- 2 tablespoons rosemary, fresh
- 2 tablespoons thyme leaves, fresh
- 2 tablespoons sage, fresh
- 2 tablespoons lemon zest, fresh
- 4 flounder fillets
- sea salt & black pepper to taste

DIRECTIONS:

1. Ready your oven to 350, and then put all of the ingredients except for the flounder in the processor. Blend until it forms at hick paste. Put your fillets on a baking sheet, and brush them down with the paste. Allow them to chill in the fridge for an hour. Bake for ten minutes. Season and serve warm.

Nutrition (for 100g): 307 calories 11g fats 7g carbohydrates 34g protein 824mg sodium

CAULIFLOWER QUINOA

Preparation Time : 15 minutes

Cooking Time : 10 minutes

Servings : 4

Difficulty Level : Easy

INGREDIENTS:

- 1 1/2 cups quinoa, cooked
- 3 tablespoons olive oil
- 3 cups cauliflower florets
- 2 spring onions, chopped
- 1 tablespoon red wine vinegar
- sea salt & black pepper to taste
- 1 tablespoon red wine vinegar
- 1 tablespoon chives, chopped
- 1 tablespoon parsley, chopped

DIRECTIONS:

1. Start by heating up a pan over medium-high heat. Add your oil. Once your oil is hot, add in your spring onions and cook for about two minutes. Add in your quinoa and cauliflower, and then add in the rest of the ingredients. Mix well, and cover. Cook for nine minutes over medium heat, and divide between plates to serve.

Nutrition (for 100g): 290 calories 14g fats 9g carbohydrates 26g protein 656mg sodium

MANGO PEAR SMOOTHIE

Preparation Time : 5 minutes

Cooking Time : 0 minutes

Servings : 1

Difficulty Level : Easy

INGREDIENTS:

- 2 ice cubes
- ½ cup Greek yogurt, plain
- ½ mango, peeled, pitted & chopped
- 1 cup kale, chopped

- 1 pear, ripe, cored & chopped

DIRECTIONS:

1. Blend together until thick and smooth. Serve chilled.

Nutrition (for 100g): 350 calories 12g fats 9g carbohydrates 40g protein 457mg sodium

SPINACH OMELET

Preparation Time : 10 minutes

Cooking Time : 20 minutes

Servings : 4

Difficulty Level : Easy

INGREDIENTS:

- 3 tablespoons olive oil
- 1 onion, small & chopped
- 1 clove garlic, minced
- 4 tomatoes, large, cored & chopped
- 1 teaspoon sea salt, fine
- 8 eggs, beaten
- ¼ teaspoon black pepper
- 2 ounces feta cheese, crumbled
- 1 tablespoon flat leaf parsley, fresh & chopped

DIRECTIONS:

1. Preheat oven to 400 degrees, and pour olive oil in an ovenproof skillet. Place your skillet over high heat, adding in your onions. Cook for five to seven minutes. Your onions should soften.
2. Add your tomatoes, salt, pepper and garlic in. Then simmer for another five minutes, and fill in your beaten eggs. Mix lightly, and cook for three to five minutes. They should set at the bottom. Put the pan in the oven, baking for five minutes more. Remove from the oven, topping with parsley and feta. Serve warm.

Nutrition (for 100g): 280 calories 19g fats 10g carbohydrates 31g protein 625mg sodium

ALMOND PANCAKES

Preparation Time : 15 minutes

Cooking Time : 15 minutes

Servings : 6

Difficulty Level : Easy

INGREDIENTS:

- 2 cups almond milk, unsweetened & room temperature

- 2 eggs, large & room temperature

- ½ cup coconut oil, melted + more for greasing

- 2 teaspoons honey, raw

- ¼ teaspoon sea salt, fine

- ½ teaspoon baking soda

- 1 ½ cups whole wheat flour

- ½ cup almond flour

- 1 ½ teaspoons baking powder

- ¼ teaspoon cinnamon, ground

DIRECTIONS:

1. Get out a large bowl and whisk your coconut oil, eggs, almond milk and honey, blending until it's mixed well.

2. Get a medium bowl out and sift together your baking powder, baking soda, almond flour, sea salt, whole wheat flour and cinnamon. Mix well.

3. Add your flour mixture to your milk mixture, and whisk well.

4. Get out a large skillet and grease it using your coconut oil before placing it over medium-high heat. Add in your pancake batter in ½ cup measurements.

5. Cook for three minutes or until the edges are firm. The bottom of your pancake should be golden, and bubbles should break the surface. Cook both sides.

6. Wipe clean your skillet, and repeat until all of your batter is used. Make sure to re-grease your skillet, and top with fresh fruit if desired.

Nutrition (for 100g): 205 calories 16g fats 9g carbohydrates 36g protein 828mg sodium

TOMATO SALAD

Preparation Time : 20 minutes

Cooking Time : 0 minutes

Servings : 4

Difficulty Level : Easy

INGREDIENTS:

- 1 cucumber, sliced

- ¼ cup sun dried tomatoes, chopped

- 1 lb. tomatoes, cubed

- ½ cup black olives

- 1 red onion, sliced

- 1 tablespoon balsamic vinegar
- ¼ cup parsley, fresh & chopped
- 2 tablespoons olive oil
- sea salt & black pepper to taste

DIRECTIONS:

1. Get out a bowl and combine all of your vegetables together. To make your dressing mix all your seasoning, olive oil and vinegar. Toss with your salad and serve fresh.

Nutrition (for 100g): 126 Calories 2g Fat 5g Carbohydrates 1g Protein 681mg Sodium

FETA BEET SALAD

Preparation Time : 15 minutes

Cooking Time : 0 minutes

Servings : 4

Difficulty Level : Easy

INGREDIENTS:

- 6 red beets, cooked & peeled
- 3 ounces feta cheese, cubed
- 2 tablespoons olive oil
- 2 tablespoons balsamic vinegar

DIRECTIONS:

1. Combine everything together, and then serve.

Nutrition (for 100g): 230 Calories 12g Fat 3g Carbohydrates 3g Protein 614mg Sodium

CAULIFLOWER & TOMATO SALAD

Preparation Time : 15 minutes

Cooking Time : 0 minutes

Servings : 4

Difficulty Level : Easy

INGREDIENTS:

- 1 head cauliflower, chopped
- 2 tablespoons parsley, fresh & chopped
- 2 cups cherry tomatoes, halved
- 2 tablespoons lemon juice, fresh
- 2 tablespoons pine nuts

- sea salt & black pepper to taste

DIRECTIONS:

1. Mix your lemon juice, cherry tomatoes, cauliflower and parsley together, and then season. Top with pine nuts, and mix well before serving.

Nutrition (for 100g): 64 Calories 3g Fat 9g Carbohydrates 8g Protein 614mg Sodium

PILAF WITH CREAM CHEESE

Preparation Time : 20 minutes

Cooking Time : 10 minutes

Servings : 6

Difficulty Level : Average

INGREDIENTS:

- 2 cups yellow long grain rice, parboiled

- 1 cup onion

- 4 green onions

- 3 tablespoons butter

- 3 tablespoons vegetable broth

- 2 teaspoons cayenne pepper

- 1 teaspoon paprika

- ½ teaspoon cloves, minced

- 2 tablespoons mint leaves, fresh & chopped

- 1 bunch fresh mint leaves to garnish

- 1 tablespoons olive oil

- sea salt & black pepper to taste

- Cheese Cream:

- 3 tablespoons olive oil

- sea salt & black pepper to taste

- 9 ounces cream cheese

DIRECTIONS:

1. Ready the oven at 360 degrees, and then pull out a pan. Heat your butter and olive oil together, and cook your onions and spring onions for two minutes.

2. Add in your salt, pepper, paprika, cloves, vegetable broth, rice and remaining seasoning. Sauté for three minutes. Wrap with foil, and bake for another half hour. Allow it to cool.

3. Mix in the cream cheese, cheese, olive oil, salt and pepper. Serve your pilaf garnished with fresh mint leaves.

Nutrition (for 100g): 364 Calories 30g Fat 20g Carbohydrates 5g Protein 511mg Sodium

ROASTED EGGPLANT SALAD

Preparation Time : 10 minutes
Cooking Time : 20 minutes
Servings : 6
Difficulty Level : Easy
INGREDIENTS:

- 1 red onion, sliced
- 2 tablespoons parsley, fresh & chopped
- 1 teaspoon thyme
- 2 cups cherry tomatoes, halved
- sea salt & black pepper to taste
- 1 teaspoon oregano
- 3 tablespoons olive oil
- 1 teaspoon basil
- 3 eggplants, peeled & cubed

DIRECTIONS:

1. Start by heating your oven to Season your eggplant with basil, salt, pepper, oregano, thyme and olive oil. Situate it on a baking tray, and bake for a half hour. Toss with your remaining ingredients before serving.

Nutrition (for 100g): 148 Calories 7g Fat 5g Carbohydrates 5g Protein 660mg Sodium

ROASTED VEGGIES

Preparation Time : 5 minutes
Cooking Time : 15 minutes
Servings : 12
Difficulty Level : Easy
INGREDIENTS:

- 6 cloves garlic
- 6 tablespoons olive oil
- 1 fennel bulb, diced
- 1 zucchini, diced
- 2 red bell peppers, diced

- 6 potatoes, large & diced
- 2 teaspoons sea salt
- ½ cup balsamic vinegar
- ¼ cup rosemary, chopped & fresh
- 2 teaspoons vegetable bouillon powder

DIRECTIONS:

1. Start by heating your oven to Put your potatoes, fennel, zucchini, garlic and fennel on a baking dish, drizzling with olive oil. Sprinkle with salt, bouillon powder, and rosemary. Mix well, and then bake at 450 for thirty to forty minutes. Mix your vinegar into the vegetables before serving.

Nutrition (for 100g): 675 Calories 21g Fat 112g Carbohydrates 13g Protein 718mg Sodium

PISTACHIO ARUGULA SALAD

Preparation Time : 20 minutes

Cooking Time : 0 minutes

Servings : 6

Difficulty Level : Easy

INGREDIENTS:

- 6 cups kale, chopped
- ¼ cup olive oil
- 2 tablespoons lemon juice, fresh
- ½ teaspoon smoked paprika
- 2 cups arugula
- 1/3 cup pistachios, unsalted & shelled
- 6 tablespoons parmesan cheese, grated

DIRECTIONS:

1. Get out a salad bowl and combine your oil, lemon, smoked paprika and kale. Gently massage the leaves for half a minute. Your kale should be coated well. Gently mix your arugula and pistachios when ready to serve.

Nutrition (for 100g): 150 Calories 12g Fat 8g Carbohydrates 5g Protein 637mg Sodium

PARMESAN BARLEY RISOTTO

Preparation Time : 10 minutes

Cooking Time : 20 minutes

Servings : 6

Difficulty Level : Difficult

INGREDIENTS:

- 1 cup yellow onion, chopped
- 1 tablespoon olive oil
- 4 cups vegetable broth, low sodium
- 2 cups pearl barley, uncooked
- ½ cup dry white wine
- 1 cup parmesan cheese, grated fine & divided
- sea salt & black pepper to taste
- fresh chives, chopped for serving
- lemon wedges for serving

DIRECTIONS:

1. Add your broth into a saucepan and bring it to a simmer over medium-high heat. Get out a stock pot and put it over medium-high heat as well. Heat your oil before adding in your onion. Cook for eight minutes and stir occasionally. Add in your barley and cook for two minutes more. Stir in your barley, cooking until it's toasted.

2. Pour in the wine, cooking for a minute more. Most of the liquid should have evaporated before adding in a cup of warm broth. Cook and stir for two minutes. Your liquid should be absorbed. Add in the remaining broth by the cup, and cook until ach cup is absorbed. It should take about two minutes each time.

3. Pull out from the heat, add half a cup of cheese, and top with remaining cheese, chives, and lemon wedges.

Nutrition (for 100g): 345 Calories 7g Fat 56g Carbohydrates 14g Protein 912mg Sodium

SEAFOOD & AVOCADO SALAD

Preparation Time : 10 minutes

Cooking Time : 0 minutes

Servings : 4

Difficulty Level : Easy

INGREDIENTS:

- 2 lbs. salmon, cooked & chopped
- 2 lbs. shrimp, cooked & chopped
- 1 cup avocado, chopped
- 1 cup mayonnaise
- 4 tablespoons lime juice, fresh
- 2 cloves garlic

- 1 cup sour cream
- sea salt & black pepper to taste
- ½ red onion, minced
- 1 cup cucumber, chopped

DIRECTIONS:

1. Start by getting out a bowl and combine your garlic, salt, pepper, onion, mayonnaise, sour cream and lime juice,
2. Get out a different bowl and mix together your salmon, shrimp, cucumber, and avocado.
3. Add the mayonnaise mixture to your shrimp, and then allow it to sit for twenty minutes in the fridge before serving.

Nutrition (for 100g): 394 Calories 30g Fat 3g Carbohydrates 27g Protein 815mg Sodium

MEDITERRANEAN SHRIMP SALAD

Preparation Time : 40 minutes

Cooking Time : 0 minutes

Servings : 6

Difficulty Level : Easy

INGREDIENTS:

- 1 ½ lbs. shrimp, cleaned & cooked
- 2 celery stalks, fresh
- 1 onion
- 2 green onions
- 4 eggs, boiled
- 3 potatoes, cooked
- 3 tablespoons mayonnaise
- sea salt & black pepper to taste

DIRECTIONS:

1. Start by slicing your potatoes and chopping your celery. Slice your eggs, and season. Mix everything together. Put your shrimp over the eggs, and then serve with onion and green onions.

Nutrition (for 100g): 207 Calories 6g Fat 15g Carbohydrates 17g Protein 664mg Sodium

GREEK FISH SOUP

Preparation Time : 10 minutes

Cooking Time : 60 minutes

Servings : 4

Difficulty Level : Easy

INGREDIENTS:

- Hake or other white fish
- 4 Potatoes
- 4 Spring onions
- 2 Carrots
- 2 stalks of Celery
- 2 Tomatoes
- 4 tablespoons Extra virgin olive oil
- 2 Eggs
- 1 Lemon
- 1 cup Rice
- Salt to taste

DIRECTIONS:

1. Choose a fish not exceeding 2pounds in weight, remove its scales, gills and intestines and wash it well. Salt it and set aside.
2. Wash the potatoes, carrots and onions and put them in the saucepan whole with enough water to soak them and then bring to a boil.
3. Add in the celery still tied in bunches so it does not disperse while cooking, cut the tomatoes into four parts and add these too, together with oil and salt.
4. When the vegetables are almost cooked, add more water and the fish. Boil for 20 minutes then remove it from the broth together with the vegetables.
5. Place the fish in a serving dish by adorning it with the vegetables and strain the broth. Put the broth back on the heat, diluting it with a little water. Once it boils, put in the rice and season with salt. Once the rice is cooked, remove the saucepan from the heat.
6. Prepare the avgolemono sauce:
7. Beat the eggs well and slowly add the lemon juice. Put some broth in a ladle and slowly pour it into the eggs, mixing constantly.
8. Finally, add the obtained sauce to the soup and mix well.

Nutrition (for 100g): 263 Calories 1g Fat 6g Carbohydrates 9g Protein 823mg Sodium

VENERE RICE WITH SHRIMP

Preparation Time : 10 minutes

Cooking Time : 55 minutes

Servings : 3

Difficulty Level : Easy

INGREDIENTS:

- 1 ½ cups of black Venere rice (better if parboiled)
- 5 teaspoons extra virgin olive oil
- 5oz shrimp
- 5oz zucchini
- 1 Lemon (juice and rind)
- Table Salt to taste
- Black pepper to taste
- 1 clove garlic
- Tabasco to taste

DIRECTIONS:

1. Let's start with the rice:
2. After filling a pot with plenty of water and bringing it to a boil, pour in the rice, add salt, and cook for the necessary time (check the package's cooking instructions).
3. Meanwhile, grate the zucchini with grater with large holes. In a pan, heat the olive oil with the peeled garlic clove, add the grated zucchini, salt and pepper, and cook for 5 minutes, remove the garlic clove and set the vegetables aside.
4. Now clean the shrimp:
5. Remove the shell, cut the tail, divide them in half lengthwise, and remove the intestine (the dark thread in their back). Situate the cleaned shrimps in a bowl and season with olive oil; give it some extra flavor by adding lemon zest, salt and pepper and by adding a few drops of Tabasco if you so choose.
6. Heat up the shrimps in a hot pan for a couple of minutes. Once cooked, set aside.
7. Once the Venere rice is ready, strain it in a bowl, add the zucchini mix and stir.

Nutrition (for 100g): 293 Calories 5g Fat 52g Carbohydrates 10g Protein 655mg Sodium

BAKED BEAN FISH MEAL

Preparation Time : 10 minutes

Cooking Time : 10 minutes

Servings : 4

Difficulty Level : Easy

INGREDIENTS:

- 1 tablespoon balsamic vinegar
- 2 ½ cups green beans
- 1-pint cherry or grape tomatoes
- 4 (4-ounce each) fish fillets, such as cod or tilapia

- 2 tablespoons olive oil

DIRECTIONS:

1. Preheat an oven to 400 degrees. Grease two baking sheets with some olive oil or olive oil spray. Arrange 2 fish fillets on each sheet. In a mixing bowl, pour olive oil and vinegar. Combine to mix well with each other.
2. Mix green beans and tomatoes. Combine to mix well with each other. Combine both mixtures well with each other. Add mixture equally over fish fillets. Bake for 6-8 minutes, until fish opaque and easy to flake. Serve warm.

Nutrition (for 100g): 229 Calories 13g Fat 8g Carbohydrates 5g Protein 559mg Sodium

MUSHROOM COD STEW

Preparation Time : 10 minutes

Cooking Time : 20 minutes

Servings : 6

Difficulty Level : Easy

INGREDIENTS:

- 2 tablespoons extra-virgin olive oil
- 2 garlic cloves, minced
- 1 can tomato
- 2 cups chopped onion
- ¾ teaspoon smoked paprika
- a (12-ounce) jar roasted red peppers
- 1/3 cup dry red wine
- ¼ teaspoon kosher or sea salt
- ¼ teaspoon black pepper
- 1 cup black olives
- 1 ½ pounds cod fillets, cut into 1-inch pieces
- 3 cups sliced mushrooms

DIRECTIONS:

1. Get medium-large cooking pot, warm up oil over medium heat. Add onions and stir-cook for 4 minutes. Add garlic and smoked paprika; cook for 1 minute, stirring often. Add tomatoes with juice, roasted peppers, olives, wine, pepper, and salt; stir gently. Boil mixture. Add the cod and mushrooms; turn down heat to medium. Close and cook until the cod is easy to flake, stir in between. Serve warm.

Nutrition (for 100g): 238 Calories 7g Fat 15g Carbohydrates 5g Protein 772mg Sodium

MUSTARD TROUT WITH APPLES

Preparation Time : 15 minutes

Cooking Time : 55 minutes

Servings : 2

Difficulty Level : Difficult

INGREDIENTS:

- 1 Tablespoon Olive Oil
- 1 Small Shallot, Minced
- 2 Lady Apples, Halved
- 4 Trout Fillets, 3 Ounces Each
- 1 1/2 Tablespoons Bread Crumbs, Plain & Fine
- 1/2 Teaspoon Thyme, Fresh & Chopped
- 1/2 Tablespoon Butter, Melted & Unsalted
- 1/2 Cup Apple Cider
- 1 Teaspoon Light Brown Sugar
- 1/2 Tablespoon Dijon Mustard
- 1/2 Tablespoon Capers, Rinsed
- Sea Salt & Black Pepper to Taste

DIRECTIONS:

1. Prepare oven to 375 degrees, and then get out a small bowl. Combine your bread crumbs, shallot and thyme before seasoning with salt and pepper.

2. Add in the butter, and mix well.

3. Put the apples cut side up in a baking dish, and then sprinkle with sugar. Top with bread crumbs, and then pour half of your cider around the apples, covering the dish. Bake for a half an hour.

4. Uncover, and then bake for twenty more minutes. The apples should be tender but your crumbs should be crisp. Remove the apples from the oven.

5. Turn the broiler on, and then put the rack four inches away. Pat your trout down, and then season with salt and pepper. Brush your oil on a baking sheet, and then put your trout with the skin side up. Brush your remaining oil over the skin, and broil for six minutes. Repeat the apples on the shelf right below the trout. This will keep the crumbs from burning, and it should only take two minutes to heat up.

6. Get out a saucepan, and whisk your remaining cider, capers, and mustard together. Add more cider if necessary, to thin, and cook for five minutes on medium-high. It should have a sauce like consistency. Scoop the juices over the fish, and serve with an apple on each plate.

Nutrition (for 100g): 366 calories 13g fats 10g carbohydrates 31g protein 559mg sodium

GNOCCHI WITH SHRIMP

Preparation Time : 5 minutes

Cooking Time : 15 minutes

Servings : 4

Difficulty Level : Difficult

INGREDIENTS:

- 1/2 lb. Shrimp, Peeled & Deveined
- 1/4 Cup Shallots, Sliced
- 1/2 Tablespoon + 1 Teaspoon Olive Oil
- 8 Ounces Shelf Stable Gnocchi
- 1/2 Bunch Asparagus, Cut into Thirds
- 3 Tablespoons Parmesan Cheese
- 1 Tablespoon Lemon Juice, Fresh
- 1/3 Cup Chicken Broth
- Sea Salt & Black Pepper to Taste

DIRECTIONS:

1. Start by heating a half a tablespoon of oil over medium heat, and then add in your gnocchi. Cook while stirring often until they turn plump and golden. This will take from seven to ten minutes. Place them in a bowl.
2. Heat your remaining teaspoon of oil with your shallots, cooking until they begin to brown. Make sure to stir, but this will take two minutes. Stir in the broth before adding your asparagus. Cover, and cook for three to four minutes.
3. Add the shrimp, seasoning with salt and pepper. Cook until they are pink and cooked through, which will take roughly four minutes.
4. Return the gnocchi to the skillet with lemon juice, cooking for another two minutes. Stir well, and then remove it from heat.
5. Sprinkle with parmesan, and let it stand for two minutes. Your cheese should melt. Serve warm.

Nutrition (for 100g): 342 calories 11g fats 9g carbohydrates 38g protein 711mg sodium

SHRIMP SAGANAKI

Preparation Time : 15 minutes

Cooking Time : 30 minutes

Servings : 2

Difficulty Level : Average

INGREDIENTS:

- 1/2 lb. Shrimp with Shells
- 1 Small Onion, Chopped
- 1/2 Cup White Wine
- 1 Tablespoon Parsley, Fresh & Chopped
- 8 Ounces Tomatoes, Canned & Diced
- 3 Tablespoons Olive Oil
- 4 Ounces Feta Cheese
- Cubed Salt
- Dash Black Pepper
- 14 Teaspoon Garlic Powder

DIRECTIONS:

1. Get out a saucepan and then pour in about two inches of water, bringing it to a boil. Boil for five minutes, and then drain but reserve the liquid. Set both the shrimp and the liquid to the side.
2. Heat two tablespoons of oil up next, and when heated add in your onions. Cook until the onions are translucent. Mix in your parsley, garlic, wine, olive oil and tomatoes. Simmer for a half hour, and stir until it's thickened.
3. Remove the legs of the shrimp, pulling off the shells, head and tail. Add the shrimp and shrimp stock into the sauce once it's thickened. Bring it to a simmer for five minutes, and then add the feta cheese. Let it stand until the cheese starts to melt, and then serve warm.

Nutrition (for 100g): 329 calories 14g fat 10g carbohydrates 31g protein 449mg sodium

MEDITERRANEAN SALMON

Preparation Time : 10 minutes

Cooking Time : 20 minutes

Servings : 2

Difficulty Level : Easy

INGREDIENTS:

- 2 Salmon Fillets, Skinless & 6 Ounces Each
- 1 Cup Cherry Tomatoes
- 1 Tablespoon Capers
- 1/4 Cup Zucchini, Chopped Fine
- 1/8 Teaspoon Black Pepper
- 1/8 Teaspoon Sea Salt, Fine
- 1/2 Tablespoon Olive Oil

- 25 Ounces Ripe Olives, Sliced

DIRECTIONS:

1. Ready the oven to 425 degrees, and then sprinkle your salt and pepper over your fish on both sides. Place the fish in a single layer on your baking dish after coating your baking dish using cooking spray.
2. Combine the tomatoes and remaining ingredients, spooning the mixture over your fillets, and then bake for twenty-two minutes. Serve warm.

Nutrition (for 100g): 322 calories 10g fats 15g carbohydrates 31g protein 493mg sodium

HOT AND FRESH FISHY STEAKS

Preparation Time : 14 minutes

Cooking Time : 14 minutes

Servings : 2

Difficulty Level : Easy

INGREDIENTS:

- Garlic, 1 clove, minced
- Lemon juice, 1 tablespoon
- Brown sugar, 1 tablespoon
- Halibut steak, 1 pound
- Salt and pepper to taste
- Soy sauce, ¼ teaspoon
- Butter, 1 teaspoon
- Greek yogurt, 2 tablespoons

DIRECTIONS:

1. Over a medium flame, preheat the grill. Mix the butter, sugar, yogurt, lemon juice, soy sauce and seasonings in a bowl. Warm the mixture in a pan. Use this mixture to brush onto the steak while cooking on the griller. Serve hot.

Nutrition (for 100g): 412 Calories 4g Fat 6g Carbohydrates 11g Protein 788mg Sodium

MUSSELS O' MARINE

Preparation Time : 20 minutes

Cooking Time : 10 minutes

Servings : 2

Difficulty Level : Easy

INGREDIENTS:

- Mussels, scrubbed and debearded, 1 pound

- Coconut milk, ½ cup

- Cayenne pepper, 1 teaspoon

- Fresh lemon juice, 1 tablespoon

- Garlic, 1 teaspoon, minced

- Cilantro, freshly chopped for topping

- Brown sugar, 1 teaspoon

DIRECTIONS:

1. Mix all the ingredients, except the mussels in a pot. Heat the mixture and bring it to the boil. Add the mussels, and cook for 10 minutes. Serve in a dish with the boiled liquid.

Nutrition (for 100g): 483 Calories 4g Fat 6g Carbohydrates 2g Protein 499mg Sodium

SLOW COOKER MEDITERRANEAN BEEF ROAST

Preparation Time : 10 minutes

Cooking Time : 10 hours and 10 minutes

Servings : 6

Difficulty Level : Average

INGREDIENTS:

- 3 pounds Chuck roast, boneless

- 2 teaspoons Rosemary

- ½ cup Tomatoes, sun-dried and chopped

- 10 cloves Grated garlic

- ½ cup Beef stock

- 2 tablespoons Balsamic vinegar

- ¼ cup Chopped Italian parsley, fresh

- ¼ cup Chopped olives

- 1 teaspoon Lemon zest

- ¼ cup Cheese grits

DIRECTIONS:

1. In the slow cooker, put garlic, sun dried tomatoes, and the beef roast. Add beef stock and Rosemary. Close the cooker and slow cook for 10 hours.

2. After cooking is over, remove the beef, and shred the meet. Discard the fat. Add back the shredded meat to the slow cooker and simmer for 10 minutes. In a small bowl combine lemon zest, parsley, and olives. Cool the mixture until you are ready to serve. Garnish using the refrigerated mix.

3. Serve it over pasta or egg noodles. Top it with cheese grits.

SLOW COOKER CHICKEN CASSOULET

Preparation Time : 10 minutes

Cooking Time : 20 minutes

Servings : 16

Difficulty Level : Average

INGREDIENTS:

- 1 cup dry navy beans, soaked
- 8 bone-in skinless chicken thighs
- 1 Polish sausage, cooked and chopped into bite-sized pieces (optional)
- 1¼ cup tomato juice
- 1 (28-ounce) can halved tomatoes
- 1 tbsp Worcestershire sauce
- 1 tsp instant beef or chicken bouillon granules
- ½ tsp dried basil
- ½ teaspoon dried oregano
- ½ teaspoon paprika
- ½ cup chopped celery
- ½ cup chopped carrot
- ½ cup chopped onion

DIRECTIONS:

1. Brush the slow cooker with olive oil or nonstick cooking spray. In a mixing bowl, stir together the tomato juice, tomatoes, Worcestershire sauce, beef bouillon, basil, oregano, and paprika. Make sure the ingredients are well combined.
2. Place the chicken and sausage into the slow cooker and cover with the tomato juice mixture. Top with celery, carrot, and onion. Cook on low for 10–12 hours.

Nutrition (for 100g): 244 Calories 7g Fat 25g Carbohydrates 21g Protein 736mg Sodium

SLOW COOKER CHICKEN PROVENCAL

Preparation Time : 5 minutes

Cooking Time : 8 hours

Servings : 4

Difficulty Level : Easy

INGREDIENTS:

- 4 (6-ounce) skinless bone-in chicken breast halves
- 2 teaspoons dried basil
- 1 teaspoon dried thyme
- 1/8 teaspoon salt
- 1/8 teaspoon freshly ground black pepper
- 1 yellow pepper, diced
- 1 red pepper, diced
- 1 (5-ounce) can cannellini beans
- 1 (5-ounce) can petite tomatoes with basil, garlic, and oregano, undrained

DIRECTIONS:

1. Brush the slow cooker with nonstick olive oil. Add all the ingredients to the slow cooker and stir to combine. Cook on low for 8 hours.

Nutrition (for 100g): 304 Calories 5g Fat 3g Carbohydrates 4g Protein 639mg Sodium

GREEK STYLE TURKEY ROAST

Preparation Time : 20 minutes

Cooking Time : 7 hours and 30 minutes

Servings : 8

Difficulty Level : Average

INGREDIENTS:

- 1 (4-pound) boneless turkey breast, trimmed
- ½ cup chicken broth, divided
- 2 tablespoons fresh lemon juice
- 2 cups chopped onion
- ½ cup pitted Kalamata olives
- ½ cup oil-packed sun-dried tomatoes, thinly sliced
- 1 teaspoon Greek seasoning
- ½ teaspoon salt
- ¼ teaspoon fresh ground black pepper
- 3 tablespoons all-purpose flour (or whole wheat)

DIRECTIONS:

1. Brush the slow cooker with nonstick cooking spray or olive oil. Add the turkey, ¼ cup of the chicken broth, lemon juice, onion, olives, sun-dried tomatoes, Greek seasoning, salt and pepper to the slow cooker.

2. Cook on low for 7 hours. Scourge the flour into the remaining ¼ cup of chicken broth, then stir gently into the slow cooker. Cook for an additional 30 minutes.

Nutrition (for 100g): 341 Calories 19g Fat 12g Carbohydrates 4g Protein 639mg Sodium

GARLIC CHICKEN WITH COUSCOUS

Preparation Time : 25 minutes

Cooking Time : 7 hours

Servings : 4

Difficulty Level : Average

INGREDIENTS:

- 1 whole chicken, cut into pieces
- 1 tablespoon extra-virgin olive oil
- 6 cloves garlic, halved
- 1 cup dry white wine
- 1 cup couscous
- ½ teaspoon salt
- ½ teaspoon pepper
- 1 medium onion, thinly sliced
- 2 teaspoons dried thyme
- 1/3 cup whole wheat flour

DIRECTIONS:

1. Cook the olive oil in a heavy skillet. When skillet is hot, add the chicken to sear. Make sure the chicken pieces don't touch each other. Cook with the skin side down for about 3 minutes or until browned.
2. Brush your slow cooker with nonstick cooking spray or olive oil. Put the onion, garlic, and thyme into the slow cooker and sprinkle with salt and pepper. Stir in the chicken on top of the onions.
3. In a separate bowl, whisk the flour into the wine until there are no lumps, then pour over the chicken. Cook on low for 7 hours or until done. You can cook on high for 3 hours as well. Serve the chicken over the cooked couscous and spoon sauce over the top.

Nutrition (for 100g): 440 Calories 5g Fat 14g Carbohydrates 8g Protein 674mg Sodium

CHICKEN KARAHI

Preparation Time : 5 minutes

Cooking Time : 5 hours

Servings : 4

Difficulty Level : Easy

INGREDIENTS:

* 2 lbs. chicken breasts or thighs
* ¼ cup olive oil
* 1 small can tomato paste
* 1 tablespoon butter
* 1 large onion, diced
* ½ cup plain Greek yogurt
* ½ cup water
* 2 tablespoons ginger in garlic paste
* 3 tablespoons fenugreek leaves
* 1 teaspoon ground coriander
* 1 medium tomato
* 1 teaspoon red chili
* 2 green chilies
* 1 teaspoon turmeric
* 1 tablespoon garam masala
* 1 teaspoon cumin powder
* 1 teaspoon sea salt
* ¼ teaspoon nutmeg

DIRECTIONS:

1. Brush the slow cooker with nonstick cooking spray. In a small bowl, thoroughly mix all of the spices. Mix in the chicken to the slow cooker, followed by the ingredients' rest, including the spice mixture. Stir until everything is well mixed with the spices.
2. Cook on low for 4–5 hours. Serve with naan or Italian bread.

Nutrition (for 100g): 345 Calories 9g Fat 10g Carbohydrates 7g Protein 715mg Sodium

CHICKEN CACCIATORE WITH ORZO

Preparation Time : 20 minutes

Cooking Time : 4 hours

Servings : 6

Difficulty Level : Easy

INGREDIENTS:

* 2 pounds skin-on chicken thighs
* 1 tablespoon olive oil
* 1 cup mushrooms, quartered

- 3 carrots, chopped
- 1 small jar Kalamata olives
- 2 (14-ounce) cans diced tomatoes
- 1 small can tomato paste
- 1 cup red wine
- 5 garlic cloves
- 1 cup orzo

DIRECTIONS:

1. In a large skillet, cook the olive oil. When the oil is heated, add the chicken, skin side down, and sear it. Make sure the pieces of chicken don't touch each other.
2. When the chicken is browned, add to the slow cooker along with all the ingredients except the orzo. Cook the chicken on low for 2 hours, then add the orzo and cook for an additional 2 hours. Serve with a crusty French bread.

Nutrition (for 100g): 424 Calories 16g Fat 10g Carbohydrates 11g Protein 845mg Sodium

5-INGREDIENT ZUCCHINI FRITTERS

Preparation Time : 15 minutes
Cooking Time : 5 minutes
Servings : 14
Difficulty Level : Average
INGREDIENTS:

- 4 cups grated zucchini
- Salt, to taste
- 2 large eggs, slightly beaten
- 1/3 cup sliced scallions
- 2/3 all-purpose flour
- 1/8 teaspoon black pepper
- 2 tablespoons olive oil

DIRECTIONS:

1. Situate the grated zucchini in a colander and lightly season with salt. Set aside to rest for 10 minutes. Grip as much liquid from the grated zucchini as possible.
2. Pour the grated zucchini into a bowl. Fold in the beaten eggs, scallions, flour, salt, and pepper and stir until everything is well combined.
3. Heat up the olive oil in a large skillet over medium heat until hot.
4. Drop 3 tablespoons mounds of the zucchini mixture onto the hot skillet to make each fritter, pin them

lightly into rounds and spacing them about 2 inches apart.

5. Cook for 2 to 3 minutes. Flip the zucchini fritters and cook for 2 minutes more, or until they are golden brown and cooked through.

6. Remove from the heat to a plate lined with paper towels. Repeat with the remaining zucchini mixture. Serve hot.

Nutrition (for 100g): 113 Calories 1g Fat 9g Carbohydrates 4g Protein 793mg Sodium

MOROCCAN TAGINE WITH VEGETABLES

Preparation Time : 20 minutes

Cooking Time : 40 minutes

Servings : 2

Difficulty Level : Average

INGREDIENTS:

- 2 tablespoons olive oil
- ½ onion, diced
- 1 garlic clove, minced
- 2 cups cauliflower florets
- 1 medium carrot, cut into 1-inch pieces
- 1 cup diced eggplant
- 1 can whole tomatoes with juices
- 1 (15-ounce / 425-g) can chickpeas
- 2 small red potatoes
- 1 cup water
- 1 teaspoon pure maple syrup
- ½ teaspoon cinnamon
- ½ teaspoon turmeric
- 1 teaspoon cumin
- ½ teaspoon salt
- 1 to 2 teaspoons harissa paste

DIRECTIONS:

1. In a Dutch oven, heat up the olive oil over medium-high heat. Sauté the onion for 5 minutes, stirring occasionally, or until the onion is translucent.

2. Stir in the garlic, cauliflower florets, carrot, eggplant, tomatoes, and potatoes. Mash tomatoes by using a wooden spoon into smaller pieces.

3. Add the chickpeas, water, maple syrup, cinnamon, turmeric, cumin, and salt and stir to incorporate. Let

it boil

4. Once done, reduce the heat to medium-low. Stir in the harissa paste, cover, allow to simmer for about 40 minutes, or until the vegetables are softened. Taste and adjust seasoning as needed. Let it rest before serving.

Nutrition (for 100g): 293 Calories 9g Fat 1g Carbohydrates 2g Protein 811mg Sodium

FIGS PIE

Preparation Time : 10 minutes
Cooking Time : 60 minutes
Servings : 8
Difficulty Level : Average
INGREDIENTS:

- ½ cup stevia
- 6 figs, cut into quarters
- ½ teaspoon vanilla extract
- 1 cup almond flour
- 4 eggs, whisked

DIRECTIONS:

1. Spread the figs on the bottom of a springform pan lined with parchment paper. In a bowl, combine the other ingredients, whisk and pour over the figs. Bake at 375 digress F for 1 hour, flip the pie upside down when it's done and serve.

Nutrition (for 100g): 200 Calories 4g Fat 6g Carbohydrates 8g Protein 351mg Sodium

CHERRY CREAM

Preparation Time : 2 hours
Cooking Time : 0 minutes
Servings : 4
Difficulty Level : Easy
INGREDIENTS:

- 2 cups cherries, pitted and chopped
- 1 cup almond milk
- ½ cup whipping cream
- 3 eggs, whisked
- 1/3 cup stevia
- 1 teaspoon lemon juice

- ½ teaspoon vanilla extract

DIRECTIONS:

1. In your food processor, combine the cherries with the milk and the rest of the ingredients, pulse well, divide into cups and keep in the fridge for 2 hours before serving.

Nutrition (for 100g): 200 Calories 5g Fat 6g Carbohydrates 4g Protein 278mg Sodium

STRAWBERRIES CREAM

Preparation Time : 10 minutes

Cooking Time : 20 minutes

Servings : 4

Difficulty Level : Easy

INGREDIENTS:

- ½ cup stevia
- 2 pounds strawberries, chopped
- 1 cup almond milk
- Zest of 1 lemon, grated
- ½ cup heavy cream
- 3 egg yolks, whisked

DIRECTIONS:

1. Heat up a pan with the milk over medium-high heat, add the stevia and the rest of the ingredients, whisk well, simmer for 20 minutes, divide into cups and serve cold.

Nutrition (for 100g): 152 Calories 4g Fat 1g Carbohydrates 8g Protein 361mg Sodium

APPLES AND PLUM CAKE

Preparation Time : 10 minutes

Cooking Time : 40 minutes

Servings : 4

Difficulty Level : Average

INGREDIENTS:

- 7 ounces almond flour
- 1 egg, whisked
- 5 tablespoons stevia
- 3 ounces warm almond milk
- 2 pounds plums, pitted and cut into quarters

- 2 apples, cored and chopped
- Zest of 1 lemon, grated
- 1 tsp baking powder

DIRECTIONS:

1. Blend well the almond milk with the egg, stevia, and the rest of the ingredients except the cooking spray
2. Grease a cake pan with the oil, pour the cake mix inside, introduce in the oven at 350 degrees F for 40 minutes.
3. Cool down, slice and serve.

Nutrition (for 100g): 209 Calories 4g Fat 8g Carbohydrates 6g Protein281mg Sodium

CINNAMON CHICKPEAS COOKIES

Preparation Time : 10 minutes

Cooking Time : 20 minutes

Servings : 12

Difficulty Level : Average

INGREDIENTS:

- 1 cup canned chickpeas
- 2 cups almond flour
- 1 teaspoon cinnamon powder
- 1 teaspoon baking powder
- 1 cup avocado oil
- ½ cup stevia
- 1 egg, whisked
- 2 teaspoons almond extract
- 1 cup raisins
- 1 cup coconut, unsweetened and shredded

DIRECTIONS:

1. In a bowl, combine the chickpeas with the flour, cinnamon and the other ingredients, and whisk well until you obtain a dough.
2. Scoop tablespoons of dough on a baking sheet lined with parchment paper, introduce in oven for 20 minutes at 350 degrees. Let it cool and serve.

Nutrition (for 100g): 200 Calories 5g Fat 5g Carbohydrates 4g Protein 311mg Sodium

COCOA BROWNIES

Preparation Time : 10 minutes

Cooking Time : 20 minutes

Servings : 8

Difficulty Level : Average

INGREDIENTS:

- 30 ounces canned lentils, rinsed and drained
- 1 tablespoon honey
- 1 banana, peeled and chopped
- ½ teaspoon baking soda
- 4 tablespoons almond butter
- 2 tablespoons cocoa powder
- Cooking spray

DIRECTIONS:

1. In a food processor, pulse well the lentils with the honey and the other ingredients except the cooking spray.
2. Transfer this into a pan greased with cooking spray, lay evenly, introduce in the oven at 375 degrees F for 20 minutes. Slice the brownies and serve cold.

Nutrition (for 100g): 200 Calories 5g Fat 7g Carbohydrates 3g Protein 252mg Sodium

CARDAMOM ALMOND CREAM

Preparation Time : 30 minutes

Cooking Time : 0 minutes

Servings : 4

Difficulty Level : Easy

INGREDIENTS:

- Juice of 1 lime
- ½ cup stevia
- 1 and ½ cups water
- 3 cups almond milk
- ½ cup honey
- 2 teaspoons cardamom, ground
- 1 teaspoon rose water
- 1 teaspoon vanilla extract

DIRECTIONS:

1. In a blender, blend well the almond milk with the cardamom and the rest of the ingredients, divide into

cups and keep in the fridge for 30 minutes before serving.

Nutrition (for 100g): 283 Calories 8g Fat 7g Carbohydrates 1g Protein 321mg Sodium

BANANA CINNAMON CUPCAKES

Preparation Time : 10 minutes

Cooking Time : 20 minutes

Servings : 4

Difficulty Level : Easy

INGREDIENTS :

- 4 tablespoons avocado oil
- 4 eggs
- ½ cup orange juice
- 2 teaspoons cinnamon powder
- 1 teaspoon vanilla extract
- 2 bananas, peeled and chopped
- ¾ cup almond flour
- ½ teaspoon baking powder
- Cooking spray

DIRECTIONS:

1. In a bowl, combine the oil with the eggs, orange juice and the other ingredients except the cooking spray, whisk well, pour in a cupcake pan greased with the cooking spray. Introduce in oven for 20 minutes, at 350 degrees F.
2. Cool the cupcakes down and serve.

Nutrition (for 100g): 142 Calories 8g Fat 7g Carbohydrates 6g Protein 214mg Sodium

RHUBARB AND APPLES CREAM

Preparation Time : 10 minutes

Cooking Time : 0 minutes

Servings : 6

Difficulty Level : Easy

INGREDIENTS:

- 3 cups rhubarb, chopped
- 1 and ½ cups stevia
- 2 eggs, whisked

- ½ teaspoon nutmeg, ground
- 1 tablespoon avocado oil
- 1/3 cup almond milk

DIRECTIONS:

1. In a blender, combine the rhubarb with the stevia and the rest of the ingredients, pulse well, divide into cups and serve cold.

Nutrition (for 100g): 200 Calories 2g Fat 6g Carbohydrates 5g Protein

ALMOND RICE DESSERT

Preparation Time : 10 minutes

Cooking Time : 20 minutes

Servings : 4

Difficulty Level : Easy

INGREDIENTS:

- 1 cup white rice
- 2 cups almond milk
- 1 cup almonds, chopped
- ½ cup stevia
- 1 tablespoon cinnamon powder
- ½ cup pomegranate seeds

DIRECTIONS:

1. In a pot, incorporate the rice with the milk and stevia, bring to a simmer and cook for 20 minutes, stirring often. Add the rest of the ingredients, stir, divide into bowls and serve.

Nutrition (for 100g): 234 Calories 5g Fat 4g Carbohydrates 5g Protein 317mg Sodium

MEDITERRANEAN BAKED APPLES

Preparation Time : 5 minutes

Cooking Time : 25 minutes

Servings : 4

Difficulty Level : Easy

INGREDIENTS:

- 5 pounds apples, peeled and sliced
- Juice from ½ lemon
- A dash of cinnamon

DIRECTIONS:

1. Preheat the oven to 2500 F. Line a baking sheet with parchment paper then set aside. In a medium bowl, apples with lemon juice and cinnamon. Place the apples on the parchment paper-lined baking sheet. Bake for 25 minutes until crisp.

Nutrition (for 100g): 90 Calories 3g Fat 9g Carbohydrates 5g Protein 633mg Sodium

CHIA ALMOND BUTTER PUDDING

Preparation Time : 5 minutes

Cooking Time : 10 minutes

Servings : 1

Difficulty Level : Easy

INGREDIENTS:

- ¼ cup chia seeds
- 1 cup unsweetened almond milk
- 1 ½ tablespoons maple syrup
- 2 ½ tablespoons almond butter

DIRECTIONS:

1. Add almond milk, maple syrup, and almond butter in a bowl and stir well. Add chia seeds and stir to mix. Pour pudding mixture into the Mason jar and place it in the refrigerator overnight. Serve and enjoy.

Nutrition (for 100g): 354 Calories 3g Fat 1g Carbohydrates 2g Protein 251mg Sodium

SWEET RICE PUDDING

Preparation Time : 10 minutes

Cooking Time : 30 minutes

Servings : 4

Difficulty Level : Average

INGREDIENTS:

- 1 ¼ cup of rice
- ¼ cup dark chocolate, chopped
- 1 teaspoon vanilla
- 1/3 cup coconut butter
- 1 teaspoon liquid stevia
- 2 ½ cup almond milk

DIRECTIONS:

1. Incorporate all ingredients inside the inner pot and mix well. Cover and cook on high for 20 minutes. Once done, allow to release pressure naturally. Remove lid. Stir well and serve.

Nutrition (for 100g): 638 Calories 9g Fat 5g Carbohydrates 6g Protein 354mg Sodium

CREAMY YOGURT BANANA BOWLS

Preparation Time : 15 minutes

Cooking Time : 0 minutes

Servings : 4

Difficulty Level : Easy

INGREDIENTS:

- 2 bananas, sliced
- ½ teaspoon ground nutmeg
- 3 tablespoon flaxseed meal
- ¼ cup creamy peanut butter
- 4 cups Greek yogurt

DIRECTIONS:

1. Divide Greek yogurt between 4 serving bowls and top with sliced bananas. Add peanut butter in microwave-safe bowl and microwave for 30 seconds.

2. Drizzle 1 tablespoon of melted peanut butter on each bowl on top of the sliced bananas. Sprinkle cinnamon and flax meal on top and serve.

Nutrition (for 100g): 351 Calories 1g Fat 6g Carbohydrates 6g Protein 322mg Sodium